MATH

FROM TEARS TO SMILES

A Parent's Guide

Why math matters, why so many kids
struggle with it and when to intervene
to turn math anxiety into
ACADEMIC SUCCESS

FEENIX PAN, Ph.D.

MATH: From Tears to Smiles

ISBN Paperback: 978-0-578-81408-7
ISBN eBook: 978-0-578-67323-3

From Tears to Smiles Press Tucson, AZ
www.fromtearstosmiles.com

Printed in the United States

TO THE
light, love and joy
IN ALL OF US

Also

in memory of

Dr. Wozny (1931–2019)
Pioneer in Childhood Education

Dr. Shack (1927–2019)
Inventor, Professor, and Mentor

and Fanya (1940–2020)

CONTENTS

FOREWORD

I first learned of Dr. Feenix Pan's excellence as a mathematics instructor when I, as the Science, Technology, Engineering, and Mathematics Division Dean at our local community college, reviewed the student evaluations for her course. All were complimentary, praising her for how she made the course relevant to real-life; some comments were even gushing, which was unusual for a math class. During her tenure at the college, Dr. Pan was a very popular faculty member and her classes filled quickly. I was saddened when she left to focus on her new business venture: Door-2-Math. Little did I know that within a few years, I would be asking Dr. Pan to help our daughter improve her *MathAbility*.

"I suck at math." How I hated hearing our daughter say this every evening as she struggled to complete her fourth-grade homework. "That's not how my teacher does it!" She would protest as I tried to help. One day, my husband and I experienced a "Time Warp" moment as we watched in horror as she demonstrated how to multiply two-digit numbers; she performed a modified cross-multiplication with a jump-to-the-left "dance:"[1]

---

[1] With apologies to Sharman, J., O'Brien, R., White, M., Curry, T., Sarandon, S., Bostwick, B., Quinn, P., Twentieth Century Fox Home Entertainment, Inc. (1975). *The Rocky Horror picture show.* Beverly Hills, Calif: Twentieth Century Fox Home Entertainment.

$$\begin{array}{r} 79 \\ \times\ \underline{99} \\ 63 \\ +\ \underline{81} \\ 873 \end{array}$$

She clearly had no concept of the place value of the digits in a number! How could this be? Math skills were something we took for granted in our family.

"What is 79 times 10?" my husband asked.

"790," she answered.

"What is 79 times 100?" he continued gently.

"7900," she answered without hesitation.

"So how in the world could 79 times 99, which is almost like 79 times 100, be anywhere close to 873?" I blurted out.

She started to cry. "I don't know, I hate math!"

Several such evenings ensued, some of which escalated into full-blown math wars, and after poor grades on her first quarter report card, my husband and I grew terrified that career doors would be closing for her. We decided to turn to a professional.

Dr. Feenix Pan immediately came to mind. Our daughter took an instant liking to Dr. Pan, who allowed her to take breaks when she needed them and rewarded her efforts with praise. Prior to the fourth grade, our daughter had used her incredible memory to succeed in arithmetic. Now, the mechanics of the operations she was required to do were a bit more complicated, word problems were more challenging, and estimation skills would have been helpful. We marveled as Dr. Pan built upon our daughter's best ways of learning, helped her design an ideal physical setting for doing her homework, and tapped into her innate critical thinking abilities and desire for self-reliance. Her math skills and confidence rapidly improved, and she also developed better organizational skills.

A key breakthrough occurred one afternoon as Dr. Pan observed me helping our daughter. In a non-judgmental voice, she commented, "You were leaning into your daughter's space and then you took the pencil from her hand." I instantly became mindful of my own impatience and frustration. It was a watershed moment that helped me become a better guide for our child and ultimately, a better parent.

And what became of that once-frustrated fourth grader, you may wonder? She earned her bachelor's degree in science and will complete a master's degree, also in science, this year. My husband and I could not be prouder of her achievements and know that we owe a great debt of gratitude to Dr. Pan who taught us how to unlock our daughter's potential. Hopefully, she will be able to help you to do the same for your child.

Ann Christensen, Ph.D., M.Div.

Dean of Science, Technology, Engineering, and Mathematics
(Retired)
Pima Community College

CHAPTER 1

Why This Book

Dear parents,

If a child in your life is struggling with math and test anxiety, you may feel lost, bewildered, hopeless, or even in despair. But please be encouraged.

Hi, I'm Dr. Feenix Pan, and since 2003 I have been teaching and coaching kids to recover from math and test anxiety and helping them to realize their full academic potential. If you want to know more about my background right away, skip ahead and take a look at Chapter Two.

I invite you to consider this book as a practical guide to help a child navigate the landscape of K–12 math with ease. This book does not teach you math. Instead, it details a process that I have developed while working with hundreds of kids and their families, on how *you, the parent,* can influence a child's lifelong relationship with math *regardless of your own math level*. It is my sincere hope that after reading this book you will be able to manage math-related conflicts, hear your child's unspoken words, and impart methods of effective and efficient learning to your child, all in a way that maintains and strengthens that special bond you share with a child. In this book, I share with you the same journey that I've been sharing with other parents: to help each family raise resilient, empowered, strong, and thriving kids by transforming their relationship with math from tears to smiles. When a child's math skills, learning abilities, and confidence improve, so usually do their grades, their joy in learning, family harmony, their college options, and their career possibilities.

Five insights and a unique process from 17 years in the trenches as a performance coach

1. Math is different from all other subjects in that it's the most difficult to keep up with. This is because of its sequential nature. With most other subjects, there are many places you can start from, and the information fits together like an expanding puzzle. Math, however, builds upon itself from the foundation of counting and addition all the way to calculus in the twelfth grade. A gap in understanding *at any part* of the math sequence will weaken understanding of all that follows. That gap is like a sinkhole under the math highway, and the more pressure put on it, the worse the collapse.

2. More than any other subject, the level of math understanding achieved by senior year in high school will influence a child's potential career and college choices. I'm not saying I approve of this—it's just the way it is. Many educational and career tracks are not available to kids who cannot pass college math entrance exams at a higher level.

3. In most cases it is the parents' or guardians' responsibility, rather than the school's, to manage kids' math education. Why? Because even the best schools work for the interest of the school, not individual children. This may sound harsh but if you think about it, schools have budgets, limited resources, and a new batch of kids coming in every year. Schools are evaluated by kids' test scores, not the level of understanding that they achieve. Teachers are under intense pressure to promote kids to the next grade even when they are not ready. I've seen many cases where kids are promoted from grade to grade, yet their math levels are years behind. Later on in

this book, I'll show you ways to tell if a child is falling behind in math, even if their grades say otherwise.

4. YOU are essential to a child's math success. Every child with math and test anxiety needs at least one adult in their life who believes in them. Love matters. Faith matters. Change takes time and effort. When you cherish a child's potential, you help make that potential real for the child and for the world.

5. There are many ways to help and effectively guide kids on their math journey that do not require you to be a math genius.

Parents often confuse responsibility with capacity. Responsibility is your ability to respond, whereas capacity is your ability to teach. Sometimes parents who are good at math struggle *more* to teach their kids math. This can be frustrating for everyone involved, especially the parents. (Believe me, I have had those difficulties myself with both of my own kids.) Other parents, who have struggled with math themselves, are at a loss and tend to pass on their math fears and insecurities. Whether you are someone who uses math professionally, or someone who gave up on math in the fifth grade, or you fall somewhere in between, you've probably tried many ways to help — whether it's sitting down with their math homework, finding a math tutor, or locating resources online. If you've experienced only moderate success with these strategies, or if any progress made was non-lasting, this is quite common.

This is why this book is not about teaching math nor helping you to teach your child math, rather it's to help you change the way you respond through a process. This process has proven extremely effective with the parents and kids I've worked with. I call this process **Math And Managing MathAbility—MAMMA** for short. By MathAbility, I refer to *a set of four core learning skills, **separate** from math concepts, that each kid needs to develop to be academically successful. These skills include: organization skills, ability to formulate effective questions and ask for help from adults, test-taking skills, and critical thinking skills.*

MAMMA: a process of transforming math tears to math smiles

My own math struggles started in 1978 when I was in second grade in rural China. I'll describe all that in the next chapter so that you know that I do understand what it means to struggle with math. But first, let's fast forward to 2003. By this time, I'd earned three advanced degrees: two master's and a Ph.D., all in science and engineering. It was my own childhood struggle with math and the ultimate triumph that started me on the path of developing the MAMMA process. I am now a full-time educational consultant and performance coach. I spend most of my days working with parents who find themselves in a math war with a battle-scarred child handicapped by math and test anxiety and often low self-esteem.

Helping any child with math becomes increasingly challenging as math concepts get denser. *The problem parents have is seldom lack of effort; rather, it's lack of an accurate assessment on how kids best learn and of a coherent plan for smoothly progressing kids through the benchmarks of the K–12 math curriculum.* Instead of putting a band-aid on a bleeding situation (teaching parents the math concepts or how to teach their child math), core underlying *learning issues* need to first be promptly and properly addressed. The MAMMA process detailed in this book is the result of my work with this new approach.

In a nutshell, the MAMMA process uses the 80-20 rule, where 20 percent is about the actual math concepts and 80 percent is *not* about math concepts. Instead, 80 percent is about helping parents develop a new understanding of the unique way math works, along with the knowledge of building and managing MathAbility. Because these learning skills are outside of math concepts, *any* caring and patient adult can work toward passing them onto a child in their life.

Part of building and managing MathAbility is to get clear on your own strengths and thoroughly reassess your assumptions about math and learning. This may sound off-topic or too much trouble for some parents, but it is essential and very liberating. Remember, building and managing

MathAbility is not about helping a child get a quick "A" on *one* math test. It is a practical process for helping parents acquire the right mindset to assist a child in *becoming* a skillful lifelong learner.

One caveat: I do not claim, with the MAMMA process, that all my parent-clients morph into successful educators-in-chief overnight. Some families quit for one reason or another before completing the program: some have many other competing priorities. As an educator and coach, I can tell you that no matter how hard I try to impart knowledge and learning habits to a child while working with them, I can never transform a child the way *you* can. Why? Because *your* child lives in an environment created by *your* awareness, *your* perspective, and *your* personal values.

When you help your child through something as challenging as math and test anxiety, the confidence of everyone involved skyrockets. Once your child experiences what it's like to learn with joy and ease, they realize they don't have to shy away from other demanding subjects, and the effects are truly magical and delightful. The child comes to cherish lifelong learning and seeks to express their learning in ways that are meaningful to them. This is why I want to share the MAMMA process with as many families as possible.

In the next chapter, I'll tell you my story. You'll learn about my math struggles, what helped me to overcome them, how becoming a mom changed my perspective, and how I became a performance coach—an accidental math guru of sorts.

CHAPTER 2

Tears and Scars: My Math Story

The greatest risk is risking a riskless living.
—Leo Buscaglia

"One pair of shoes to share", Circa 1973   *Graduating class, circa 1985*

I was born in a mud hut in a tiny farming village in northern China, about 700 miles from Beijing. Both sets of grandparents held government posts before 1949. When the Communist Party took over, both families were demoted from city to countryside during the Chinese Cultural Revolution, and in the late 1960s, when China experienced one of its infamous famines, I lost three grandparents. But as a kid growing up in rural China, my younger brother and I were quite happy with chasing chickens and goats alongside other older village kids, even if we were poor and shared only one pair of shoes.

My dad worked as a truck driver and a part-time mechanic. My earliest memories involve me accompanying him as he fixed trucks on farms. I was probably three years old. I remember farmers giving me fresh milk from cows—a delicious luxury back then, only I'd throw it all up. Years later I found out I am lactose intolerant.

A hard worker, my dad kept getting better and better at fixing trucks and tractors. In 1978, after the government lifted the ban on higher education, he passed some national tests and was admitted into a university in Beijing. So off he went. I was almost seven that year. A few years later, he passed more exams and then attended a university in the United States.

After he left for school, my mom raised us by herself while holding down a teaching job and pursuing a college degree in education. This meant that we had to move a lot, and it was difficult for me to find a niche among other kids, as the social cliques had already formed in every school I attended.

My struggle with math started early

Before my dad left for Beijing, our first move took us from the countryside to a small town. There was no daycare available for my younger brother. Desperate, my parents shuffled me into second grade so my brother could take the only available first grade slot. The kids in my class were much older, and they were far ahead of me. They were studying the multiplication table. Right away, I couldn't keep up. One day my math teacher lost her temper and threw a textbook at me. It missed my eye, but left scars on my forehead right above my right eyebrow. That was when math went from *hard* to *scary*. I fell further and further behind. And that was only second grade.

For the next six years, I floundered. My dad was overseas, and my mom was overworked. When I turned thirteen, my mom moved us to a larger city. She enrolled herself in a night school for a teaching degree and tried to get me transferred into a new high school. By then, I was failing most of my science classes and math (of course), and this school refused to take any transfer students with mediocre grades.

I remember thinking: *This is the worst feeling ever.* It was one thing to flunk math and pretend not to care, but it was altogether different to be rejected because of failing grades. I found myself locked outside of the school's gate. I was an outsider in the most literal sense.

I felt ashamed, rejected, and defeated. But this experience, terrible as it was, was invaluable. It taught me that if I let one subject stop me from learning, I could end up having nowhere to go and no one to talk to.

My mom didn't have the money to pay the backchannels to get me in as a regular student. Thank goodness a math teacher took pity, broke some rules and put me on academic probation as a boarding student who "earns" her spot. I lived in a dorm with seven other girls, all of us "work-study" students. Most of them, like me, had failing math and science grades. We all got up at 5 a.m. to do chores: wiping the desks, sweeping the schoolyard, and in the winter, starting the fire stoves for the classrooms before other students arrived.

My first year as a boarding student was rough, but for the first time in years, I *wanted* to learn. Still, math classes were horribly difficult. Every homework problem was a trap, an occasion for headaches, and humiliation.

Yet the fear of being kicked out of school felt far more painful. I didn't want to end up outside of the school gate again, so I made a math chart with all the concepts I had no clue about, and started to work through them. First on my own, and when that didn't work, I camped outside my math teacher's office.

With his help, it became clear that I learned in pictures and was very much a *visual learner* (a foreign concept for me back then). Up until that point, most of the math instruction was spoken and it made no sense to me. Patiently, my teacher helped me work through concepts I didn't understand with pages and pages of pictures and graphics. Once I accidentally misplaced a decimal point while solving a word problem in front of the class, which made the cost of an egg almost ten times more than its actual cost. But my teacher didn't laugh at me. Instead, he brought the entire class to a market the next day and showed us that the cost of a whole chicken was less than the "golden egg" I'd calculated the day before. Under his guidance, I gradually improved. Within a year and a half, I was admitted as a regular student and started to enjoy my newfound math freedom.

But when we immigrated to the United States a few years later, the progress I had made all but evaporated. I turned sixteen that year. It was quite a culture shock when we landed in South Dakota, where my dad got his first teaching job.

This time I was an outsider *and* a foreigner.

I didn't realize it back then, but that was another valuable experience because I learned to tolerate being different. I'm not saying I enjoyed the feeling, it's just that I got used to it. And today I can tolerate it when my approach to problem solving is different. I learned to see and tackle problems using different tools from two very different cultures.

At this new American high school, with a new language and a new culture to learn, I was losing ground fast. Once again, I sat down and tackled math, this time with the help of my Chinese-English dictionary. I would bang my head against a problem for hours, getting more and more frustrated, hating the material.

One night I fell asleep on top of my textbook while preparing for a math test the next day. When I woke up the next morning, I didn't have enough time to finish my homework, so I used the time I had to redo the chapter examples over and over. That turned out to be one of the most efficient and effective ways to learn math. Seeing how to solve *one* problem correctly showed me how to solve others like it. After that, I started to look for patterns in learning math, and I practiced hard at it.

You may say, "We are told 'practice makes perfect.' Why would that surprise you?"

But it is not just practice, practice, practice. It's practicing the *right thing*. Practicing the wrong thing and getting no result is demoralizing.

Because high school teenagers can be pretty harsh when picking on a foreigner's pronunciation and vocabulary, I started to write short sentences on index cards and string them together to make conversation. It turns out that *this* technique is essential for building mastery in math, and it's called chunking,[2] as I found out years later. It's an advanced technique, and not one that many teachers demonstrate in class.

What came of my math struggle

I finished high school in Wisconsin after another family move, and then I enrolled at the college where my dad was an associate professor in the Electrical Engineering department. I had thought of pursuing a degree in writing, but my dad advised me not to go into the writing program because English was my second language. So my undergraduate degree was in Electrical Engineering and my two master's degrees were in Optical Sciences and Electrical Engineering.

As I got deeper into higher math, I felt more and more strongly that there is a process for figuring out *how to learn math*, and that such a process would be a great tool for building confidence and ensuring future career possibilities, *especially for school-aged kids*. Then something happened to put my feelings and ideas to the test.

I was finishing up my doctoral research on space telescopes at the University of Arizona and was on track to become an academic or scientist at NASA. On the day I finished defending my thesis, my advisor came over to congratulate me. He shook my hand and said, "Let me be the first one to shake your hand, *Dr.* Pan."

At that precise moment, I felt a cold knot form in the pit of my stomach. I did not want to spend *forty to fifty years* designing space telescopes.

---

[2] B. Oakley and T. Sejnowski, *Learning How to Learn* (New York: Tarcher Perigee, 2018).

So I did the best thing a scared, uncertain, and overly educated person could do. I went to a seminar on what to do when you're scared, uncertain, and overly educated. I couldn't face the prospect of becoming a tenure-track professor, like my dad, or a government scientist as my professors had recommended. At the seminar, I ran into Erin, a friend from the University of Arizona. Out of the blue, in the middle of a seminar break, she asked me to help her with her math.

Erin's situation was a bit sticky. She explained that she had been admitted to Duke University for her MBA, but only if she could pass the math entrance exam. Their exam was slightly below the Calculus I level; she was failing Algebra I and was some five courses behind.

I thought to myself: *Why not? I'm not doing anything productive anyway.*

Within five minutes of sitting down with Erin, I knew what she was stuck on, what she needed to work on, and how to get her there without wasting four or five semesters of math that she'd never use or see again. *It was as if I had developed math fins to swim in the shark-infested math waters.* So I shared with Erin what I had figured out with my own math struggles. Within three months, Erin went from failing Algebra I to passing her entrance exam at Duke University with flying colors.

Meanwhile, a wonderful job opportunity opened up at NASA to design space telescopes. But I left it untouched, because the stirring within me was so strong that all I wanted was to share what I had learned with more Erins. I wanted to develop a teaching methodology, based on years of working through my own math struggles and anxiety, and to combine that with the help I had received so many years ago from my Chinese math teacher. I wanted to share how matching learning style with teaching style is crucial to a joyous learning experience. I wanted to share the structure of mathematics, along with its logical linchpin concepts, and pass all that on to *anyone* who is seeking freedom from math struggles.

My parents and I disagreed for many years over my choice of such a risky career, but thankfully, my husband supported me. With our two toddlers in tow, Door-2-Math was born. To pay for bare living necessities,

I accepted a part-time teaching position at a local community college, where I met Dr. Ann Christensen, who you met earlier in the foreword. I dreamed of helping more Erins, and other kids like my younger self.

Looking back at those beginning years—when I had zero training or know-how in regards to running a business, when I spent more time posting "Tutor for Hire" signs than teaching—I'm grateful for the one thing that saved me: my mom's grit.

I remembered watching my mom studying under an oil lantern after a long day's work. She didn't complain that she worked as a schoolteacher to support her husband's education, all our relatives, and her own two kids. Through it all she still found a way to pursue her own education.

I learned from her that where there's a will, there *is* a way.

So I immersed myself even deeper into becoming a math guru. Two years after taking "the road less traveled," I started to get results. In the wild and joyful years that followed, my client-families made progress that sometimes seemed miraculous, but it was not. It was the culmination of parents' commitment to grow, the kids' willingness to learn and expand, and the unique Math And Managing MathAbility (MAMMA) process that I developed and am hoping to pass it on to you.

Whether you're a parent, a guardian, a sports coach, or anyone else with a school-aged child who is struggling with math and test anxiety, the MAMMA process can help.

What I am most proud of is how some of the clients I've helped are now themselves educators, engineers, and doctoral candidates. They are helping others—younger versions of themselves—succeed in school, and achieve their full academic potential.

Nowadays, I use my own math journey to decode with kids how they learn best. After decades of trying to hide my math scars from the old mud hut days, I now show them to my clients because it reminds me—and them—that math struggles and anxiety are real. The scars say: *Yes, hurt happens, but so can healing.* In 2019, I was finishing the first draft of this book when Erin called to send her fifteen-year-old niece for me to coach. A second-generation client. It felt that life had come full circle. I now understood that our deepest pain can become our greatest gift if we find the courage to follow our heart's desire to love, to hope, and to grow.

I want to help families transform childhood math struggles and anxiety. I believe that every child can succeed with math, and parents don't have to be fluent in math to help. You don't have to know or love math to raise resilient, empowered, strong, and thriving math kids. You can accomplish this by being a role model for them, by learning and sharing your life experience, and by putting the MAMMA process to use. Together, we can turn tragedy to triumph, and tears to smiles.

In the next chapter I will show you my process, so you can see what effective intervention looks like and what can come from it.

CHAPTER 3

What's Possible Behind MathDoc's Door

> *Where you stumble, there lies your treasure.*
> —*Joseph Campbell*

Some families, when they realize their child needs help with math, seek out professional help and that's when I meet them. I've been working with kids and their math since 2003. As a result, I've observed many of the ways[3] that math can go wrong for them and have learned how to help the kids and their families find their footing and unique path to their math success. After I show you what I do in this chapter, I will explain in later chapters what you can do at home regardless of your math level.

Jane's story

My client's family—mom, dad, and their daughter (I'll call her Jane)—sit tensely in my waiting room. Clients almost always seem a bit nervous the first time we meet for their MathAbility Risk Assessment (MARA). This family is here because they hope I can help rebuild the self-confidence Jane lost during two long years of battling with math anxiety.

---

[3] You can find my teaching insights on YouTube @TucsonMathDoc.

I invite them into my conference room. Jane sits with me at my big round table and her parents sit in a different part of the room to fill out a math questionnaire. It's set up this way so parents can listen in without disturbing her math assessment.

I then give Jane a few blank pieces of paper and a pencil. My assessment form is a single sheet of paper divided into three sections. The first section represents the math foundation. The second section is a bicycle wheel with spokes. The last part is the summary. Then, I write down a math problem for Jane to solve.

The first few problems are pretty easy. I'm learning the sorts of problems Jane can solve when it comes to her math foundation. Grade school math has benchmarks: addition, subtraction, multiplication, fractions, and percentages. She is showing me what she knows, and what she is comfortable with, along with how she problem-solves. I then draw a wheel with shorter and longer spokes based on Jane's strengths and weaknesses. It's the second part, the weird-looking bicycle wheel, that is the important part. It represents the strengths Jane brings to problem-solving. Any weakness makes the wheel misshapen. If the wheel is lopsided, then the math ride is bumpy for the child. The wheel image is a clear and simple representation of how Jane experiences math internally.

I follow along with Jane's logic and make marks on the weird-looking bicycle wheel. A combination of part one (math foundation benchmarks) and part two (Jane's unique learning style) gives me an idea of how to develop a comprehensive, individualized MathAbility Plan (MAP) for Jane. Together, for months to come, we will use this MAP to address both foundation gaps and learning style issues. This is how we turn Jane's weaknesses into strengths and her tears to smiles.

Most assessments last about ninety minutes, and I usually start with the multiplication table. If that is easy for them, I move on. I go as long as the child can tolerate the stress and possible embarrassment of not knowing the material. Sometimes younger kids can last twenty minutes. But, if math has become so stressful, sometimes older kids can last only five minutes. While the child wields the pencil, I ask questions that invite them to share their math and school experiences. I do this so their reactions remain largely unvarnished. I then summarize everything I learned into the third section: Here is Jane's math foundation, her learning style, and what I think we need to do for Jane's math.

Jane's parents then join us at the table. I put Jane's math assessment results on the side, and we discuss what the parents want. From the questionnaire they worked on, they share with me what their goals are, and how much outside help they've engaged with in the past.

Jane stays quiet, but she's listening intently. She looks relieved. For the first time, she understands that math has been hard for her not because she is dumb (most kids have some version of this self-blame). Jane finally gets it that there is material she missed. She gets that math is sequential. She gets that math struggle is common and that it's possible to overcome it. It's as if Jane has been stumbling around in a dark room, running into furniture that bruises her. Now, for the first time, the light switch is flipped on, and she sees why she's been hurting.

Together, Jane, her parents and I design a MathAbility Plan (MAP) for Jane. We set goals, commit to them, and then Jane and I begin the work. We fix her foundation holes—the parts of math she missed. We teach her how she learns best. We improve her test-taking skills. We help her understand that staying organized is crucial to her math success. We help her ask better and more targeted questions in class. Gradually, homework begins to make sense, and she sees what she can do herself, and what learning skills she needs to acquire to stay ahead.

Fast forward ten years: Jane emails me to say that she has graduated from Johns Hopkins University with a master's degree in engineering.

"Dr. Pan," she writes, "I just got a job offer from an engineering consulting firm in D.C. The starting salary is $76,000. *Can you believe it?* It's just like you said years ago, 'Math opens doors and gets you invited!'"

Jane is also invited to UCLA for their doctoral program in applied math.

"After much debate," Jane's mom tells me when we meet for brunch to catch up, "Jane decided to take a year off to volunteer with Engineers Without Borders before pursuing her doctoral degree at UCLA."

"She is now confident and self-assured," her mom says.

"Well done, Mama bear," I say.

The next day, a flower basket arrives in my office. It's from Jane's mom. There is only one line on the card: *POTENTIAL—thank you for turning IMPOSSIBLE to I'M POSSIBLE*.

What is possible

From my experience, there is one thing I can say with confidence: Every child can succeed in math. Better math builds stronger kids, and it can be life-transforming.

I will let some of my former clients describe how becoming good at math changed their school experiences and how they see themselves. This is what is possible for kids who have been trapped with math and test anxiety. Not every child who struggles needs a professional performance coach. Most of them just need a better learning process, and that is what *you* can help with by using the information presented in this book.

"We met with Dr. Pan and after the assessment interview, she told us that our son, although very intelligent, was stuck at a sixth-grade math level. She advised that he needs to overcome this problem before he can move forward. For the first time, someone had a diagnosis for my son's math problems, and a plan to fix it." *- parent of a tenth grader*

"It was a rough start at the beginning, but over time miracles started happening. Our son showed up with his first A in math and has not looked back since. His attitude towards math has completely changed. He is now helping his friends at school with math and his grades in other subjects have begun to dramatically improve." *- parent of an eleventh grader*

"Our daughter is a freshman at University High School and began having difficulty in Algebra II when the school year started. After a few weeks of school, her confidence and test scores had never been lower. Working with Dr. Pan, after about five weeks, Megan turned around the corner and has now received As on her past three tests, including a 97 percent and 100 percent on two most recent tests. More importantly Meghan's confidence and self-esteem have improved dramatically. Megan is now confident that she can not only succeed, but also excel, in math at University High as she is now frequently well ahead of the rest of her class in preparation and problem-solving techniques." - *Karen, mother of a ninth grader*

"Despite my learning disability, I achieved a 93 percent on my trigonometry final." - *high school senior*

"What held me back from making progress was that I had quite a few foundation holes. So my work with Dr. Pan in our weekly sessions was to fix them. After those foundation holes were fixed, we worked on test-taking and learning how I learn best. Now I'm flying in my math classes and finally on the ball after feeling lost for so long. It was so unbelievably refreshing." - *high school junior*

So here is the takeaway:

Changing the relationship with math often changes the way kids approach learning. In fact, it changes their future. Why? In part, because many opportunities and careers hinge on a strong ability to do math. But there is another reason: Most of us perceive math as difficult, if not impossible, to learn. If kids can tackle something as challenging as math and succeed at it, they will have a positive image of themselves, and that becomes their new foundation.

And when you, the adult, work through math struggle and conflicts together with your child, you gain clarity about who you are as guardians of their potential. You hear your child's unspoken words, manage math-related conflicts, and teach your child effective and efficient learning, all in a way that strengthens that special bond you have with your child.

So, what is possible for you and your family? If you cannot visualize a positive outcome *yet*, don't worry, I'll help you. Most of the parents I work with couldn't picture it right away either. At the beginning, learning math and handling academics with ease and grace were often beyond most kids' imagination too. That's because very few have ever decoded learning how to learn, and most schools don't teach that. It's a very different way of thinking about what math is, what math is for, and what learning is all about. Now let me share two questions that I share with my client-families.

Two questions that matter

I'm a TED talk enthusiast. Most days I find a juicy talk to go with my lunch and forward the ones I like to my husband. Then one day, he returned the favor and sent me a link to "Life's 3 Simple Questions."[4] In a flash, I saw that when our child-rearing-years end, parents like us are likely to ask two questions (third question omitted):

1. You want to know if you did enough to prepare your child with adequate life tools for their journey ahead. You'll want to know if you passed on the value of resilience, grit, patience, and self-respect. You will want to know: *Did I teach enough to my child?*

2. You will also wonder if you've built a strong enough bond that will last. You will want to know with certainty that your child will pick up the phone and share their ups and downs with you. You want them to know that your love, guidance, and friendship will be there for them to get through the lowest of lows. Your heart will ask: *How much of what I contributed will my child remember?*

If either of these questions ring true right now, then what has to change so that you can be happy with the answers a few years down the road? Why not use this opportunity to gain a new perspective on why math is more than just a subject in school? Why not get to the root cause of math struggle and help your child come out stronger? Why not use this seemingly difficult and challenging subject to build your child up? Why not use this struggle to teach your child about their unique learning strength? And, why not use it to work together and strengthen that special bond? Why not use it to demonstrate *when there is a will, there is a way*? Why not use it to impart skills on critical thinking, on learning how to learn, on exploring the possibility of going after impossibilities?

---

[4] Brendon Burchard: Life's 3 Simple Questions. https://youtu.be/U8LPWrbh2Gk and *Millionaire Messenger* (New York: Free Press, 2011).

I know it may require some work and it may not be an easy journey. Had I not gone through it myself—with tons of help from others along the way—I too would think it is "impossible," "too hard," or even "not worth my time." Luckily, I did follow through, and along the way, I learned how to help other families make the math journey smoother and more pleasant, and take *years* off the learning curve.

In the next chapter, I'll examine why math matters. (It might not be for the reason you think.) After that, I'll share with you what makes math difficult, why learning it is so challenging for so many kids, and what could happen if our kids' math struggles are not addressed early. I'll show you what successful math journeys look like as other families lived them. Later, I'll explain how you can help a child who is struggling with math even if you had a hard time with math yourself. In the last few chapters, I'll also share some hard-earned, practical actions from the MAMMA trenches. It's time we take back our power to shape and strengthen our kids' education future. Let's get started, shall we?

CHAPTER 4

Why Math Matters and What's Making It So Challenging to Learn for Kids

Courage is not the absence of fear, but rather the judgment that something else is more important than fear. —Ambrose Redmoon

In the past, there were many paths kids could take to be productive members of society.[5] They could learn a small base of knowledge and skills and build on those. What we know and how we use what we know is changing exponentially, and math skills are at the heart of nearly every human endeavor and activity. Being good at math really is the key that unlocks most career doors these days. Math can be one of the best vehicles to cultivate both the natural abilities kids already have and the new skills they will need. In this chapter, we will first look at nine essential skills that math helps to develop and why so many kids (and adults) find them challenging to learn and master.

---

[5] Sir Ken Robinson "Reimagine Education Conference Talk" http://transformschools.ucla.edu, and his book *Out of Our Minds* (Oxford: Capstone, 2001).

Math skills, life skills

If you ever dread answering your child's question that goes something like this: "But, Mom! Why do I need to learn this? I'll never use algebra!" Or how about this one: "You didn't like math and your life turned out okay, so why do I have to learn math?" you can truthfully answer:

*My child, it's not just about math. You are learning life skills you **will** need and **will** use, while you are learning to master math. You never know where your passion will take you, and being good at math is like having a magic carpet that carries you to places you couldn't get to any other way.*

To help my client-family when their kids ask "why math?" I start by sharing with the parents Sir Ken Robinson's TED talk and show them this list of nine skills that learning to master math can bring to them in the future.

The first important skill we learn while learning math is **critical thinking**. This is the ability to evaluate information and decide if this information is logical and makes sense. Math provides a good vehicle to practice critical thinking skills, which can then be applied to other settings. It's hard to fool someone who has strong critical thinking skills.

The second is **memory**. Math relies on strong recalling skills. Building "memory muscles" makes it easier for kids to recall anything else they need to know.

The third is **curiosity**. Curiosity propels our world forward. Kids are innately curious, and when math is taught right, it rewards curiosity. It is important not to shut down math curiosity because that restricts the ability to understand other subjects.

If curiosity is about how things *are*, **imagination** is about how things *could be*. Being able to transfer something from the imagination into the world is a remarkable achievement. Math is a powerful tool for bringing ideas to reality. Math and its concepts underpin all of our computer programs, technologies, and financial transactions. Furthermore, science, medicine, music, and art all have math embedded within them. Kids who develop their math skills see ways for math to serve their imagination. They take delight in seeing how they can build a robot, use measurements to make a tasty meal, compose a music score, or see a heartbeat on a screen.

The fifth is **learning how to learn**. This is a skill that, more than ever, we need all through our lives. The processes and skills we rely on become outdated or even obsolete, and we need to learn anew. Every stage of math is about learning new knowledge and techniques, and how to apply them without someone telling you what to do every step of the way. Math teaches kids how to be strong learners *and* self-reliant. That's two skills for the price of one!

The sixth, **knowing how to take tests**, is a skill of its own. Not all tests are math tests, but the same skills that equip you to raise your math test scores by two letter grades will improve nearly all your test scores. Being a good test-taker involves reading comprehension, catching careless mistakes, managing time, estimating, strategizing, and problem-solving. Math provides the best opportunity to master test-taking because you can know when you have found the right answer—you can check your work (unlike history tests). Precision, accuracy, and neatness all contribute to success in test-taking. Those three skills alone contribute to success in school and beyond.

The seventh is **self-reliance**. Sooner or later, every child realizes that the adults they rely on cannot always be there for them, nor solve every problem. This has a tendency to happen with math homework rather more quickly. The kids who thrive in school and in life know this, accept it, articulate their needs, and either learn how to do it themselves or get the help they need from whomever is able to assist.

The eighth is **persistence**. Kids who are able to persist in learning, even when it is difficult, build confidence and character. Math requires repeated attempts before concepts make sense. Kids who develop tenacity through math will be able to stay persistent in multiple areas of life.

And lastly, the ninth is **grit**. Persistence gets us through the tough patches; grit is what *sustains* us for our long journey. Kids who work through math, not just one night before a quiz, but nearly every night because they have a goal in mind, develop grit. And here is a paradox: when we are developing grit we may feel imprisoned, doing hard work while others are taking it easy. However the results of hard work buy us a kind of freedom we only get from developing *for ourselves* the skills that will let us write our own future and demand the salary we are worth.

None of these skills are things you can give a child or do for a child. Not every child will develop all these skills—at least, not while you're watching. But, you can create an environment that facilitates them.

As parents, we all wish to encourage a child's unique passion and gifts. Having been on both sides of math struggle, I know in my heart that it is a tragedy when a child's ability to pursue his or her passion is limited by a math deficit. In order to convert passion to a productive force, succeeding with math may well be necessary. The better grasp a child has on math, the more opportunities they have to pursue their passion. Kids who are comfortable using math will find that it opens many doors for them as adults. In sum, critical thinking, memory, curiosity, imagination, learning how to learn, test-taking skills, self-reliance, persistence, and grit are skills they can and will use all their lives. Now that we're clear on why math matters, next let's look at why most kids (and adults) often find math so challenging to learn.

Academic debt

When I first started teaching at our local community college in 2003, I was in for a shock. In front of me were driven and hard-working adults who despite the many demands on their time, showed up after work to my math class night after night. At the top of their wish list was passing math class to get a better job so they could pay off their credit card debt.

"How much credit card debt?" I asked. The answer ranged anywhere from a few thousand to fifty or sixty grand.

"What happened, if you don't mind me asking?"

"Life happened," they answered. They all thought that if they could just faithfully pay the minimum monthly payment, then one day the loan will be paid off. But the loan just got bigger month after month and year after year.

"Compound interest?" I asked.

"What's that?" they asked. The next fifteen minutes turned into an impromptu lesson on the math of compound interest. It wasn't the syllabus assignment, but it was the lesson my students wanted—and needed—and boy, were they motivated to find out how they've been taken advantage of.

Fast forward. After a few semesters of math, the same students came in and showed me their cut-up credit card or a picture of their credit card frozen in a block of ice. They'd equipped themselves with the knowledge of how compound interest snowballed their financial debt and affected their well-being. They used their new math skills to successfully manage their debt. Just as credit card debt can ruin one's financial freedom, academic debt can ruin a kid's career possibilities. *Academic debt, especially in math, starts early*.

Foundation holes

Like my adult students, many kids find math challenging and experience math struggles. At the core, this difficulty has nothing to do with anyone's intelligence. Instead, it's largely due to the inherent uniqueness of the subject itself: **math is sequential**. We simply cannot jump around as each math concept builds on the one before that. Without mastering say a key concept of fractions in fourth grade, the fifth-grade word problems on percentages will not make sense.

Math is not like other school subjects. For example, with history, you can skip around; one day you can read about the civil war, and the next day, you can jump into World War II, and it doesn't matter what order you pick it up.

Math builds on a foundation of the basic concepts of counting, addition, subtraction, multiplication, and division. And those concepts build on each other. Anytime a child misses a key concept in any of the places, they will have what I call "**a math foundation hole**." And those math foundation holes don't fix themselves. Instead, it often snowballs from there. I often work with kids in high school who are struggling with Algebra II, and we have to go back all the way to fourth grade before their math can get healthy. When kids are rushed, or pushed forward without first addressing their math foundation holes, those kids end up struggling for years and sometimes they eventually give up.

Now that you understand how math operates differently than most other school subjects and how its sequential nature can often quickly morph into foundation holes, let's go over the *six* most common obstacles that often make *learning* math demanding.

Obstacle #1: Difficulties in reading comprehension. Math and reading can seem like two totally separate subjects, but while a child can be a good reader without being good at math, children cannot be good at math without being a good reader. The first reason for this is that word problems are a big part of the math curriculum from the third grade on. If good reading skills are lacking, a child cannot comprehend word problems, and that prevents moving forward in math.

The second reason that reading comprehension matters is because math test directions are often very specific. If a child does not understand the directions, they may do good math work but still lose points because they didn't solve the right problem.

Obstacle #2: Conflicted learning culture. Sometimes, another source of conflict is a lack of respect for education. To move forward in math, respect for the teacher is essential, as is respect for math vocabulary terms, key verbs, and rules, principles, and theorems. If kids are growing up in a culture that disrespects schools, or teachers, or science, or work ethic, their eagerness to learn begins to feel like a betrayal to their culture, and many kids would rather stop learning than betray their family and friends. If there is an element of this in your child's environment, please be the one adult who celebrates their accomplishments, who is proud of their curiosity, and who encourages them to learn.

Likewise, it sometimes seems as though the adults in the math and education picture do not respect the child. When a child feels neglected by the school or a teacher, it means that the respect *you* offer that child is all the more essential. It can make all the difference.

Obstacle #3: Inadequate test-taking skills. Taking a math test isn't about speed. Somehow, maybe because of timed tests, kids get the wrong impression that faster is better. Faster isn't better. Faster leads to making more mistakes. Faster means leaving out steps. The reality is this: kids need to show their work. That way the teacher can see what concepts are passed on, *and* kids can learn to check their work for mistakes. Part of conquering math means learning to show all work, learning how to check one's work, and having neat work. Neatness is especially important on tests because the answer has to be readable for the teacher to grade it. In a later chapter I'll go over a three-step strategy for test-taking success that I teach my clients.

Obstacle #4: Inadequate study habits. There is a Chinese proverb that the elders of my village used to say: *How we do one thing is how we do everything.* What this means is that if a student keeps a neat bedroom, locker and backpack, his math homework and tests will more than likely be neat and show complete work. On the other hand, if a kid rushes through breakfast and rushes to catch the school bus, she probably rushes through homework and math tests too. Our habits permeate our behavior. It takes effort and persistence to establish good habits, and whereas careless habits will sabotage a learner, consistent good habits will usually improve grades in all subjects, not just math. On top of improving grades, good habits can also be a lifelong source of strength.

Obstacle #5: Mismatched learning and teaching styles. What is going on when there is a competent teacher and a child *still* struggles? This happens more often than most of us adults realize. And most of the time, the difficulty is a result of a mismatch between teaching and learning styles.

If a child is really struggling in math, especially if math used to be easy for them and this year, for the first time, it is unbearably difficult, there may be a mismatch between the child's natural learning style and how the math is being presented. Some of us are visual learners: we need to see math to understand it. Some of us are auditory learners: we need to hear in order to learn. Some of us need to get our hands on objects and move them around and examine them from all sides before we "get it"; we are kinesthetic learners. These are the three major learning styles, the ones that can cause the most trouble when there is a mismatch of teaching style and learning style.

If you'd like to learn more about learning styles and multiple intelligences, there is now a wealth of information online. Howard Gardener wrote the first books describing learning styles based on multiple intelligences.

I remember working with several young clients who were not visual learners—visual learners can "see" the math in a textbook illustration. They had a terrible time in fifth-grade math because they could not understand the difference in meaning between "perimeter" and "area." I got them to use their fingers to "walk around" a shape's perimeter. Since "perimeter" is a long word, it helps them to remember that perimeter is a long measurement in length. With kids who are game players, I invite them to *Minecraft* the inside of the shape to find the area. Once they understand what perimeter and area mean, they can solve the problems.

One more quick note about different learning styles in the classroom. Some kids are interpersonal or social learners—they actually learn better when they are in groups. They aren't cheating; they are cooperating, bouncing ideas off of each other and fitting insights together. They are natural team problem-solvers. Other kids prefer to be solitary and figure things out quietly on their own. If your child is the first type, it may help to arrange shared homework time with another family. If your child is a solitary learner, you may need to quiet yourself down first and then match the child's learning style in order to help with homework.

Very few kids can teach themselves math. Most of us need math teachers, and ideally, we need teachers who teach math in a way that "makes sense" to us, that matches our learning style. If there isn't a good match, look for supplementary aids that correspond to a child's learning style: a school tutor who "gets" them, online demonstrations, audio versions of math, hands-on activities, whatever gives a child a way forward. Your school or local community resources may have what you need for no extra cost.

So far, we've covered the five most common obstacles that make learning math challenging for many kids, and they are: *difficulties in reading comprehension, conflicted learning culture, inadequate test-taking skills and study habits,* and *mismatched learning and teaching styles.* Aside from these five factors, concrete versus abstract learning comes next, and it's a big one.

Obstacle #6: Concrete versus abstract learning. For the most part, how math is taught is based on how math makes sense to adults. But guess what? What seems obvious and straightforward to adults may not seem that way to kids, because adult brains work differently. Most adults have shifted to thinking in terms of abstract ideas, principles, and general rules. *That is not how young brains work, and what makes sense to adults simply doesn't make any sense to most young brains.*

Most kids are "concrete" thinkers until, on average, anywhere from ages twelve to fifteen. That doesn't mean they think about concrete, or that they are thick and slow like concrete. It means their brain needs actual objects to count, not just numbers to memorize. They need to understand what something is for, not just be told that "it will be useful later." Some kids' brains make the shift to abstract thinking at an unusually early age, and some make the shift later. But at whatever age it does happen, when it happens it can feel like magic. Suddenly, what was terribly difficult becomes easier—where before all a kid could see was a senseless jumble of random numbers, patterns now emerge.

Here is how it happened with my daughter

Our daughter had a hard time figuring out how to solve word problems at first. To her, each looked just as hard as the last one. She couldn't see any pattern, and she couldn't see which math rules to use, or why, or how. For months, math homework meant frustration, tears, and struggle.

Then one day, when we were taking a break from word problems, she dropped an ice cube from her lemonade glass onto the floor. In our triple-digit Arizona summer, that ice cube melted in front of our eyes. Remembering a science TV show she'd watched the day before she asked me, "Mom, did you know that ice, vapor, and water are all made up of H-2-O?"

Without missing a beat, I answered, "Yes, honey. It's like the three math word problems we just got through. They are the same 'H-2-O,' no matter how different they look."

And she understood. When we went back to math homework, she was excited to figure out what the word problems had in common. She was actively looking to see how solving word problems was like using heat to turn ice to water, or water to vapor.

This shift to abstract reasoning is like finding a magic key that opens math doors that used to not only be stuck shut, but locked. And the transition cannot be forced or rushed. It happens in its own time as a child's brain matures. Until it does happen, word problems and algebra can be especially hard.

Some teaching methods bridge the gap between concrete and abstract thinking, either by using pictures and objects to "act out" word problems or by teaching a reliable process like Singapore Math, which actually includes translating a word problem into a picture. If a child in your life is still at the "concrete learning" stage, any of these bridging methods may be a big help with math homework.

Struggling in math is part of the learning process for the majority of us. In the process, kids build character and develop essential skills that they will use throughout their life—not just in math class. Some struggle is inevitable, even necessary. But when such difficulty has kids in tears, something *is* wrong. It is our responsibility as adults in their lives to figure out the real causes and to use our adult discerning abilities to make learning what it should be: an adventure.

In the next chapter, I'll share with you some telltale signs of impending math struggle even before math grades take a nosedive. We'll go over three early warning signs of math struggle (especially for younger kids), and then we'll cover what happens when math struggles go beyond math itself and how it often erodes a child's self-esteem, confidence, and their relationship with you.

CHAPTER 5

What Happens When Math Struggles Are No Longer Merely About Math

"Dr. Pan, if math could speak, what would it say?"
—*a tenth grader*

Sometimes the fear and frustration at the heart of math struggles are about so much more than just math. By showing you what such friction can look and sound like, I hope you can spot when a similar problem is making it harder for a child to learn math. I'll start this chapter with two common (but subtle) telltale signs that a child's math might be in trouble before their grades take a nosedive. Then, I'll use case studies to share with you three deeper stages of math struggle that often set in when the early warning signs go unnoticed; one is from my daughter and two are incidents from past clients who needed help to rebuild and manage their kids' MathAbility. As you read these, ask yourself: Is my child also put off with learning something that isn't making sense? Are they starting to give up (stage 1), locked in a priority struggle with me (stage 2), or in a power struggle (stage 3)?

Two subtle early warning signs of math struggle

There are two common indications that a child is *starting* to struggle with math. Most kids, even many adults, don't know how to say, "I'm having trouble understanding or coping with this." But their behaviors say otherwise.

The first warning sign is **math homework starts to take too long**. This problem is the simplest to diagnose and repair. If math homework that used to take twenty minutes now takes an hour or more, then most likely math is not making sense anymore. This often starts early in middle school and usually indicates a gap in the math foundation.

The second warning sign happens when **kids start to blame the math teacher**. It is quite true that it's harder to learn when a child doesn't have a good rapport with a teacher, and it is easier to learn if they have a good relationship with their teacher. Over the course of their educational years, kids will have good teachers, bad teachers, demanding teachers, hands-off teachers, and sometimes it will be a good match and sometimes it won't. If a teacher really is behaving badly, you may need to speak with the school administration and file a complaint. But in most circumstances, the best way to help is to focus on building your child up.

When the early warning signs of math struggle go unnoticed, math grades often start to drop. And when that is not dealt with promptly, often kids' relationship with you *and* with their learning takes a turn for the worse. It can be scary, but don't panic. Knowledge and awareness can go a long way toward rebuilding your child's MathAbility.

Stage 1. LOSING INTEREST when they say, "Do I have to do math now?"

The first visible sign of a growing math struggle is when a parent hears, "Do I have to do math now?" Just like us, kids have an innate dislike for things/subjects they are losing interest in. Lack of interest leads to procrastination, and procrastination leads to avoidance which in turn leads to the rationalization of "Who needs math anyway?" or "No one else in my class is getting this, so why should I?" All the while, new math concepts are piling up, new assignments are neglected, and before long, math grades take a nosedive. Parents panic, yell at their child; the child feels bad and tries to pick up homework, but by then she has no clue how to complete it. To pacify the parents, the child tries harder to memorize formulas that no longer make any sense, fails the tests, and finally resorts to cheating or giving up altogether.

The best way to stop this domino effect is to make sure the first domino piece doesn't fall. And that, translated to the language of MathAbility, means watching out for "Do I have to do math now?" Parents need to be like Miss Clavel[6] in the *Madeline* stories: pay attention to that inner warning sense that "something is not right."

The first time I heard "Do I have to do math now?" from our daughter, my heart skipped a beat. I cried a bit that night, feeling I had somehow failed her. As silly as it may sound, I remember thinking, "There goes her dream of becoming a physician." She was only in third grade. (She's now completing a pre-med program at Washington University in St. Louis, and you'll read her own take on her math journey later.)

As it turned out, our daughter's natural learning style is kinesthetic and visually dominant, whereas her math class was being presented in a logic-dominated and auditory way. The discrepancy between her natural learning style and how the math was being taught meant she was feeling left out and left behind. Here is the five-step approach I used to rebuild her MathAbility again:

1. Give her the freedom to express herself.

2. Let her teach me. This gave me the chance to observe her natural interests and strengths and familiarize myself with her dominant learning style.

---

[6] Clara Clavel, better known as Miss Clavel is a supporting character of Ludwig Bemelmans' *Madeline* books. She is known to be wise, caring, and loving and motherly, especially toward Madeline. She teaches the girls various life lessons to help them solve their daily conflicts and gain better insights into reality.

3. Work with what she already loved. Since she dreamed of being a physician, I challenged her to problem solve and use different methods. I used these opportunities to demonstrate how mastery of math served her dream.

4. Solicit her input in designing games/activities to "get math."

5. Let her set the learning tempo as we focused on building her math foundation, from learning good math habits to test-taking.

I remember that one of the very first obstacles I encountered was helping her to master the multiplication table. Taking a cue from her visual learning style and her interest in chess, I brought out a chessboard and told her I knew, without counting, how many squares there were on the board: 64.

Wanting to check me out, she counted the squares out.

"Yes, it is 64," she announced.

Then I told her I also know 32 are white and 32 are black.

"How did you know that so quickly?" she asked.

After checking my answers, and counting again, she was puzzled. Then I gave her a water-washable marker.

"Make any square on the chessboard. I can tell you how many small chess squares you have inside it," I said.

"Without counting?" She asked.

"That's right. Without counting," I answered.

As we played with patterns on that chessboard, she gradually realized that multiplication is just patterns of addition that can be visually represented as squares (or rectangles).

By the time she was done with her squares, she had mastered seven multiplication entries on squares: $2 \times 2 = 4$, $3 \times 3 = 9$, $4 \times 4 = 16$, $5 \times 5 = 25$, $6 \times 6 = 36$, $7 \times 7 = 49$, $8 \times 8 = 64$.

Relying on a few more mathematical principles, we got through the entire multiplication table, and that turned her math around.

Stage 2. PRIORITY CONFLICTS when they say, "Math? But what about my friends?"

Sometimes math struggles are about priorities and goals. When this gets layered on top of math struggle, it becomes a compound problem. However, if everyone in the family is on the same side, even with their differences, finding a way forward can make a big difference very quickly.

Meet Anna, a ninth grader attending a local Catholic high school.

When Beth, Anna's mom, first called, she told me: "Anna loves her school and is a good kid. She is very gifted in soccer, and plays piano. Her friends and teachers adore her, but when it comes to math, my Anna withers." Beth explained that Anna "tries so hard at her homework and stays up late to study for tests, only to be crushed by falling grades over and over."

I was relieved that Anna's math had not deteriorated to the point where she fights with her parents every night.

"It must be hard for you, too, Beth," I said.

"Oh, you have no idea, Dr. Pan. Neither my husband nor I liked math in school, so we're of no help when our daughter struggles."

After getting the bare basics down, I told Beth that the good news was that Anna still cared about her math. (I'd be a lot more concerned if Anna had stopped doing her homework altogether.) I also informed Beth that what we needed to do next was to figure out which aspects of MathAbility were causing her daughter trouble.

"MathAbility, what's that?" Beth asked.

So I told Beth an analogy that I often use on the phone with parents to explain the relationship between *math* and *MathAbility*. I told her that MathAbility is a group of skills, *outside* of math concepts, that kids need to be successful with math.

"It's like this, Beth," I said. "Think of how you hold an open umbrella. The circular canopy is big and wide—sort of like the countless math concepts—whereas the folding metal frame, supported by a central rod is a group of skills that kids need to succeed with learning math."

I told her that a child needs both math *and* MathAbility to succeed, and that either one or both might be giving Anna trouble.

"And you can tell all this by giving her some tests?" Beth asked.

"Yes," I said.

Beth just voiced another common question parents ask. I further explained that the assessment would not be some standardized test with bubbles to fill, but rather a carefully designed math dialogue.

"What kind of math dialogue?" she asked.

"Well, I'll be asking Anna questions like '1/7th and 1/8th, which one is larger?' and 'Why do you think so?'"

I told Beth that I prefer this dialogue format for several reasons. For one, it'd be less threatening. For two, it'd give me a window through which I can peer inside a child's thinking process. Are they visual and think in pictures? Or are they verbal and use inventive acronyms in aid of their studies? The last reason for a dialogue format is that it'd give me the freedom to probe a certain topic deeper or skip it altogether. If a kid can derive the quadratic equation on the spot from scratch, there is no point in wasting time by asking them to complete squares.

A week later at the assessment, Anna didn't get through the third question. With tears in her eyes, she looked totally defeated. I offered a tissue to Anna as her floodgate was then wide open.

She said, "I feel so stupid when it comes to math. I mean, it's not like I don't study or anything. I do! But when it comes to tests, it's like I don't remember a thing!"

Anna shared her grief over math, her fear over her college choices down the road, and her despair over her inability to conquer the subject.

"So, can you help her, Dr. Pan?" Anna's Dad, William, spoke for the first time since the assessment began. He looked like a problem-solver who needed a solution yesterday.

"I don't know yet," I said.

I told William that as painful and unpleasant as it is to watch our kids struggle, I'd always make a point to follow my student's lead. I had the uncomfortable feeling that this family's math struggles had gotten deeper than just math. I asked the three of them if this was the first time Anna's math struggle had come up and how it had been dealt with in the family.

"Dr, Pan, *they* don't think I know they fight about my math grades, but I do. I feel awful," Anna said.

"We should have gotten professional help sooner!" Beth added.

"You're saying *my* friend that we hired didn't help?" William asked.

"Daddy, he just did the homework for me. It didn't really help me, and I got further behind."

"*Now* you tell me!" William said.

"We *tried* to tell you!" Both Anna and Beth said at the same time.

I've learned that when two parents have different communication styles or problem-solving approaches (or both), one has to be the "boss who owns the project." Problem solvers want to experiment and see what works, whereas consensus-takers prefer to "talk about it" at great length first, hoping to find an approach that seems likely to really work. The bottom line is that both parents want the same thing: to stop this "difficulty with math" from eroding a child's joy in learning. I needed a way to bring everyone together, now that they had a chance to say what was unsaid between the three of them.

"Look," I said, "you all care. Anna cares about her math. Mom cares that Anna is struggling, and Dad cares to the point that he is willing to try just about anything to fix the problem Anna is having."

I told them that, from what I've gathered so far, all the ingredients are here. All we're missing is a proven plan to systematically restore Anna's confidence. But I also need to help them to see that Anna has to own the MathAbility project if we were to move forward and help Anna build her math up again.

"So can you help, Dr. Pan?" William asked again.

"She said she doesn't know, Daddy," Anna answered for me.

"That's right, Anna," I said. "I don't know because I can only help if you let me."

By the puzzled look I knew: *This is where the future success of the project is determined. If Anna, the child, chooses to own the project and leads me to find a way to help her, we'll catch up on her math foundation, and restore her confidence in no more than six to nine months; if she hesitates, or her parents don't relinquish the ownership of rebuilding Anna's confidence back to Anna, we don't have a team yet.*

"But isn't that why we're here?" William looked more and more puzzled.

"I think Dr. Pan is trying to get Anna to own this project," Beth said (and I was).

"Well, what do you think, Anna?" I asked.

"So, Dr. Pan, are you going to help me with my homework instead of doing it for me, and teach me the stuff I've missed in the first place?" Anna asked.

I was thrilled to see Anna start to make the connection between her own lack of effective effort, her feeling lost and falling behind in math. I told them about my own math struggle.

"But how did you manage to overcome it?" Anna asked.

I shared with them that an experienced and kind teacher had taken me to the side one day and told me "there is nothing wrong with me" and "I just learn differently." I told them that first-hand experience with math struggle made me appreciate how frustrating it is not to understand math. And yet, at the same time, having conquered my own math fear, I also know what's possible out there.

"Anna," I said, "I want for you the kind of freedom I had, to pursue any career interests with curiosity, without worrying how much math might be in it."

"That's what we want for our daughter," William said.

"I know, that's what I want for my kids, too. But here is the catch—are you guys willing to work together with me to get Anna there?" I asked.

They both said YES. Having both parents on the same page, we—the three adults—now could focus on the next task at hand: Anna prioritizing her friends over the need to build up her math.

"So, how many hours of homework are we talking about, Dr. Pan?" Anna asked.

I could tell she was trying to figure out how many of her after-school social gatherings she might have to give up in order to enter some sort of agreement with me to lift the dark clouds of math that have been shrouding her confidence.

"I can definitely appreciate your apprehension, Anna," I said.

I told her that I knew learning math is like learning a new language, and as with any new skill, practice is key. Practice takes time, and so yes, Anna would have to give up an event or two or three for a while.

"Oh." Anna slouched in her chair.

From past experience, I knew one of two things would happen. *Either she would go through the pros and cons herself and choose on her own, or her parents would step in and nudge her (some parents are not so gentle with their nudging). Either way, my job in this situation is to wait.*

"But this way, Anna, math won't make you cry again," William finally spoke.

"I know we all want this for Anna," I addressed the parents. "But the project belongs to Anna because when push comes to shove, Anna has to be the one to sit down with the homework instead of hanging out with friends. And I'm guessing it's not easy to let your friends and teammates down, Anna?" Watching tears welling up in Anna's eyes, I continued, "Once or twice your friends might forgive you, but for the duration of the project, which I'm guessing is around six or nine months, that's a long time to keep on saying, 'Sorry, I can't hang out today.'"

"But sweetie, you're popular. You can always make more friends," Beth tried to assure Anna.

"And those friends who don't understand and support you are not true friends anyway!" William added.

I made a mental note to email the parents the title of a book I read on the importance of friends to a teen. I told them, from a child's perspective, friends will almost outweigh math. That is not to say overcoming math struggle is not important. It is. But to whom? Let's think this through: If you're a grown-up and have experienced "career doors slammed in your face because of math," you'd appreciate the importance of math. If you're a grown-up who loves math and has experienced the beauty and simplicity of math, of course, you'd appreciate the importance of math. But if you are a teen, like Anna, who has not experienced either the "door-shut job opportunity" or the "simplistic beauty of math," why would you want to pick overcoming a math struggle when you could be hanging out with friends? Friends share laughter, movies, and gossip with you while math makes your stomach hurt.

"Actually, Anna, friends are more important to me than math," I said.

Then I shared that when I was her age, my family immigrated to the US because of my dad's job and that one day I had lots and lots of friends—we all spoke the same language, laughed at the same jokes, teased the same group of boys—and then I was the only foreigner in a tiny college town in the middle of South Dakota.

Anna asked, "How did you survive?"

I told her that when this one boy asked me to prom, I had to look up the word "prom" in a dictionary that I carried around with me all the time.

"So, what do you think I should do?" Anna asked me.

I told Anna that, as ridiculous as it sounds, I was not going to ask her to choose math over your friends or your friends over math. Instead, I asked for her trust. I asked her to think it over on her own and trust that whatever she chose would work out in the long run. We ended the assessment, not with the parents' wish of "let's start now," but rather Anna's "thank you for letting me choose."

Anna called four days later and wanted to start rebuilding her math. She committed to working on her math foundation and her MathAbility, and to keep our project in balance with her friendships. She found that, once she began to fix the foundation of math, she actually spent less time each night doing homework, because math was beginning to make sense. So even though she "lost" some weekend time with her friends, she "made it up" weekday afternoons.

Anna didn't have big academic goals at the time. All she wanted to do was to understand math better. Yet, on the way to accomplish what *she* wanted, she discovered that she didn't have to choose between math and friendships. As math became easier, her self-confidence soared. She had the added happiness of knowing her parents were proud of her and happy for her.

If a child is at this stage of math struggle—where conflict is partly driven by balancing math skills with social needs or other priorities—it is important to follow the kids' lead and be honest with them upfront. Yes, rebuilding math will cost them some social time, but fixing math will also give back extracurricular time down the road.

To resolve this stage of struggle, *everyone* involved needs to be candid about the common goals. If a parent wants a child to be more ambitious without their agreement, right there we'll be shifting into a power struggle. So, consider first fixing the math foundation problems. Once the math foundation is back on track, and it is balanced with social activities, parents can then make the case for more ambitious goals. And here is another tip: if you want a child to really listen to you, listen to them first.

Stage 3. POWER STRUGGLE when they say, "You can't make me do math!"

John was in tenth grade, and after years of being in accelerated math programs, he fell behind. His parents were upset that after two months of working on building his MathAbility, John only got a B- for his trigonometry class. When we met for a mid-program discussion, our goal was still the same as when we started two months earlier: Reinstate John's love for math and improve his chances for college admission.

John was a bright young man, but culture clashes with his parents—both are immigrants from China—had drowned his passion for learning, and not just with math. Shouting matches with his parents had left John bitter and shut down. He'd stopped practicing his cello, even though he'd won state-wide competition awards. And he had stopped doing math homework altogether. To make the situation worse, John's math teacher had left because of personal health reasons, and with substitute teachers in charge, students were copying homework and test answers from each other.

When the four of us got settled in my conference room, I asked if I could go first. I learned that when parents started to get solely focused on grades and became somewhat impatient about the "slowness of progress," restoring the stability of the program was the top priority.

"Let me share a personal story," I started the session when John and his parents sat down with me. "I promise you guys fifteen minutes of uninterrupted attention to hear what you have to say," I told them. Then I opened a jar I reserved for this kind of meeting. Into this jar, I put a piece of paper on which I wrote "fifteen minutes to Iris." Reassured she would have the time and space to voice her opinions, John's mom, Iris, and his dad, Paul, gave me the floor.

"By all accounts, my life is going well," I started. I could tell Iris was caught off-guard. "I'm happily married with two kids. We take long vacations, and I earn a decent living doing what I love. I graduated with honors, have two master's degrees, and completed a Ph.D. in one of the top optics programs in the nation."

I paused. "But here is the thing, Iris, my parents and I have not spoken for a few years." I shared that my parents had insisted that I become either a college professor or a NASA scientist, and when their insistence became unbearable, I broke off contact with them. All three of them looked at me, puzzled (and sad, as they got what that means).

"Iris," I said, "you're losing your son's trust."

"You don't know me, my family, or our past," Iris said. "How can you be so sure?"

"Fair enough, You're right, I don't know. But what if there is a one percent chance that John breaks off all communication with you?" I said.

From months of working with John, I knew that his grades had become a point of contention at home with Iris. Unable to figure out how to get his mom to listen to him, John reacted with doing less and less homework. On top of that, he had mentioned that he no longer spent time practicing his cello—the one thing he had proclaimed as his passion.

Silence filled the room. John looked at his mom. Paul looked at his wife. I looked at the jar with a paper that had "fifteen minutes for Iris." I opened the jar and gave Iris the floor. Iris needed more than fifteen minutes to get things off her chest. But eventually, the anger and hurt were melted away by her love for her son. Beneath all the criticism John told me about, Iris was just another mom, sad and worried about the well-being of her child. As Iris' facial expression got softer, I turned to address John. The young man's head was hanging low—a sign that he finally saw what I'd been telling him for months: "Your mom doesn't hate you. She is just worried in her own way."

"John," I said, "this is your chance to re-establish communication with your mom. I hope you can see that it really is just her worry that's behind her criticism."

"I do, Dr. Pan," John said.

"Good. An apology is in order?" I asked.

Contrary to what some people think, apologizing is not a sign of weakness or lack of power. Only someone with power and choice can make a mistake. Seeing one's mistakes, and seeing one's power, means one can apologize—and mean it. But John did not move.

"If it embarrasses you to hug your mom in front of me, I'll leave the room," I offered.

When Paul came to find me again, he whispered, "Thank you, Dr. Pan."

If you're wondering why I insisted on dissolving power struggles and what that has to do with John's math future, you're not alone. At the beginning, many parents erroneously assume that math is just a lot of formulas and that homework tutoring can fix low grades. Not so.

To learn math, a kid needs frequent practice opportunities, which translates to a *desire to learn*. In John's case, he had deliberately "lost" the desire to do homework, so that failing academically would "take something away" from his mom. Her attempts to voice her worry just further fueled John's desire to keep on "taking away."

Without the desire to do homework, there was no means to patch John's foundation gaps, nor any route to learning new material. Compounding the problem, the grades he was getting were meaningless, because kids in his class were sharing answers, and the substitute teachers were just going through the motions. Better grades were all his parents used to gauge his math progress (more on this later).

When I re-joined the three of them, I pointed out that with the next semester of AP Calculus that John would be attempting, there was not just one but three obstacles ahead:

- a still-weakened math foundation;

- tougher subject material;

- very competitive classmates.

With tears in her eyes, Iris said, "If he has to fall on his face to learn this lesson."

"That will ruin his GPA and reduce his chance of admission to a good college," Paul pointed out. From the work I had already done with John, I sensed he might've just found a new desire to turn things around. I asked John to step outside with me and I looked into his eyes and asked him, "Are you committing yourself to homework, John?"

"Yes, Dr. Pan." John said.

"I have your word?" I asked.

"Yes," John promised.

"Okay, then," I said.

Back in the office, we regrouped together and took the path that "made all the difference." I asked for a promise from both John and his mom. They both gave and kept their promises. From John, I asked: "I promise to do all homework with complete effort," and from Iris: "I will only gauge John's math progress on his effort, not his grades."

Fast forward to the completion of John's program. Not only did he take the next challenging class, he achieved an A- in AP Calculus, and got accepted into his college of choice, which was what all of them truly wanted. And they stayed as a family, not estranged people blaming each other and punishing each other over some math grades.

So what have we learned so far from each of the three cases? For **math struggle stage one**, because I listened to my daughter and heard the fear and frustration behind *"Do I have to do math now?"* I spotted the initial early sign of her struggle. If your child's struggle is in this stage, trust your instinct and address the underlying learning issue right away. Don't ignore the warning sign. For my daughter, because the MathAbility Plan (MAP) fit her learning style, she quickly regained her confidence and her natural curiosity and eagerness to learn.

For **math struggle stage two**, if learning math is coming into direct conflict with social or extracurricular activities or both, be very honest about setting goals. Be sure to share long-term views and short-term views. Figure out if the math difficulties can be ameliorated by matching homework methods to learning styles, or if some piece of the math foundation is missing and needs to be mastered.

For **math struggle stage three**, when some part of math conflict is a consequence of expectations at cross purposes, not just mismatched learning and teaching styles or a weakened math foundation in basic math, it may be necessary to clear the air and get expectations in alignment with reality, then focus on what's possible. And if a family needs outside help to accomplish this, a tutor or performance coach might make a difference. Most schools will have a counselor who may be able to help as well.

If you're a parent who is seeing math defeat tightly shutting doors on your kids' future, first do not panic. To regain their confidence and preserve their freedom to pursue their dreams, you've got to be clear about your math village and your role in your child's math life.

They say that it takes a village to raise a child. Well, my village is my personal struggle with math as a youngster; my village is a kind of teacher painstakingly rebuilding my math foundation; my village is clients who trust me with rebuilding their kid's math confidence; my village is my family, friends, and colleagues patiently letting me smooth out my teaching methodology and the MAMMA process.

Now, you are *entering* my village.

In order to re-open your child's door to learning math—or prevent it from being shut in the first place—the first order of business is to get *you* to switch from "driver of math grades" to "owner of building and managing MathAbility." Building and managing MathAbility is about taking charge and creating a *favorable* learning environment, first in *your* mind, then in your child's mind, so that math can actually grow in that favorable learning environment. Sharing your own experience grows MathAbility. Being angry with your child's teacher does not. Insisting on "effort put in," not letter grades, grows MathAbility. Yelling "We've covered this very topic last night" does not.

Lead your child to "wanting to learn," and they will drink from the math river on their own free will for years to come.

How to get your child there is what building and managing MathAbility is about. Removing a child's learning barriers is what this book is about. And with students like John, bringing down power struggle barriers clears the way to his learning so math can grow. No one else but you can do this for your child. You need clarity and a proven process that works.

In the next chapter, we'll address the hot button question I hear most often from parents: "How can I help when I don't like math myself?"

CHAPTER 6

How YOU CAN Help Without Being a Genius at Math

> *All you have is what you are, and what you give.*
> *—Ursula K. Le Guin*

Let's get to the pressing question, the one I hear most frequently from parents: "How can I possibly help my child with math when I don't understand math?" Some parents say "I don't even like math, so why would my kids listen to me?" So how can you, with or without an affinity for math, help your kids learn math, do homework, and prepare for tests? We'll cover specifics in later chapters, but first, we need to bring about the right kind of awareness and support from family or mentors—in other words, adults who support and believe in a child's potential, and that is YOU. So, to address all these questions, I have a three-part answer:

Part 1. YOU know *a lot more* than you think

Parents, if you don't have an affinity for math, please don't be discouraged by what you think you don't know. What you already know is far more important, and that is your valuable life experience with skills, wisdom, and victories.

Yes, it's not easy to teach something you don't have an affinity for—math, especially. However, you *have* figured out a lot in life by turning the unknown into the known through a process we call learning. And your child can benefit tremendously when you share about overcoming your own struggles in life. For example, here is what I saw. When a fifth-grade client came in, all frustrated and rebellious against math, his mom shared with him her own struggle of learning ballet. She shared how hard it was to learn rhythm, about taping her bruised toes, about earning money for the lessons. But, she said, it was all worth it, because it made possible doing what she loved: dancing.

So while listening to his mom's story, my client perked up and asked, "Do you really believe I can do math like you figured out how to dance?" And that was the turning point of his MathAbility program. We first mapped out the work required to get him on track with math, and then we compared what he would have to do to catch up with his math to the steps his mom had taken to learn to dance. We also drew comparisons between her triumphs with dance and what he could look forward to being able to accomplish with math. His mom didn't have to help him solve math problems; she helped him to solve life.

Consider Sue Phelps, who doesn't care for swimming herself, yet her son Michael is the most decorated Olympian of all time with 28 gold medals. Or Deloris Jordan,[7] who doesn't play basketball herself, but told her young son Michael that, "It'll not be your height that's going to make you a professional basketball player" but the means to success will be found through "hard work, determination, and patience." Those parents shared and instilled the value of hard work and knew about the *best practices* in sports. They helped their kids to achieve their full potential. They focused on the process of learning and drawing from their own life experiences. They didn't have to learn the sport themselves to support their kids in mastering it.

---

[7] Deloris Jordan, *Salt in His Shoes: Michael Jordan in *Pursuit of a Dream* (New York: Simon Schuster, 2003).

So, parents, *you* have a lot of success and experience to draw upon to help a child, a lot more than you think. You figured out how to drive a car. Maybe you know how to do preventive maintenance such as checking the oil or keeping tires inflated. You get your kids to their activities. You can care for a sick loved one. You can deal with criticism at work. You can pay bills (that's math right there!) and pay taxes (more math!). You plan and prepare meals. You have a budget and manage a household (even more math!). You know *so much more* than you think.

Part 2. YOU *can* be a great role model

Kids need role models. They want to learn. They wish to succeed. When it comes to helping with math, the way adults help is first and foremost by being a role model. There are also some very specific steps you can take to help with effectiveness and efficiency, and we'll get to those in later chapters. I'll even provide checklists. But being a role model comes first.

Here is what one thirteen-year-old said about how important role models are: "I don't just learn math and writing and science from my favorite teacher, I learn how to be an adult."

Kids are actively looking for strong role models to emulate. When they don't find them, they tend to shut down. If you can remember that your kids *want* to respect you (even if they don't always act that way), that might help you remember that you have skills, and wisdom, which makes you a role model.

To help you see yourself the way your child sees you, listen to what some of my clients have shared with me about their parents and guardians:

"I love my mom. She wakes before sunrise so she can pack our lunches. She's done this for me since kindergarten, and she even put in the cutest notes in my lunch boxes every day."

"My dad taught me to respect everyone and myself. His favorite saying is: 'Never look down at anyone and never look up at anyone. Be real with everyone.'"

> *"My grandpa volunteered at animal shelters every weekend. He was the best vet in town. I want to grow up to be like him."*
>
> *"My foster parents taught me that people change, and helped me to forgive my alcoholic birth father."*

So you see, being a role model is about who you are and how you live, not about how many math concepts you happened to master.

Part 3. YOU have the power to *transform* a child's learning process and the environment without being a math genius

The third thing you can do is to be very supportive, and *deliberately* take charge of your child's learning process *and* environment. Start with simple tasks that you might already be doing: pack school bags together; check math class supplies together; help them maintain and manage workspace for their homework assignments. Then move on to invite them to share what they've learned in school with you—build their confidence and let them teach you something new. Most kids love having a chance to reverse roles and be the one who is the "expert" in charge. Observe their communication styles closely and give them a chance to show you how they are engaged in becoming an effective learner. As they teach you, they will be reminding themselves what they've learned in the classrooms, and they will often see things they didn't fully understand, especially in their math classes. In the process of explaining it to you, they often figure out what they didn't at first understand.

Now all this may call for patience on your part, especially if you happen to "see" what they are trying to figure out. Slow down, listen, and appreciate that this is all new for your child. This is their discovery. They are discovering their math for themselves; you get to discover their unique learning styles.

Let's say you did all that, then you can go one step further: help your child figure out how to ask better questions when they get stuck. For example, you can help a child go from saying, "I don't get this at all" or "Nothing is making sense!"—which is so sweeping and vague that their math teacher won't know where your kids are stuck—to saying, "I need to use these numbers, and I think this is a division problem" (or whatever they happen to be working on). "I see I need to follow this example in the book, and I think the answer will be something like this" (estimate what the right answer might be), "but I don't see how to check my next step." If you practice using math vocabulary together early and help a child learn how to articulate clear and effective questions early, I can say with complete certainty that you are helping more than you will probably ever know.

MathAbility is contagious in a good way. For example, when you help your child develop the ability to ask clear and effective questions, (one of the four core skills of MathAbility), other kids can benefit as well. When one kid figures out how to ask clear and effective questions and asks these questions in class, they are actually helping other kids. Almost certainly, some classmates got stuck in the same place, but they either don't know how to ask a clear question, or they are too shy or scared to ask it. A classmate's precise question and the teacher's explanation can help to clarify that concept for an entire class. So you see, it comes full circle. Kids want and need strong role models, and when an adult is a positive role model at home, a child becomes a role model in school.

What you can do next is to make homework time sacred; on the days your child doesn't bring homework home, use the homework time for math-related activities. This is very important, especially for younger kids. Kids who develop the habit of dedicating time *every day* to math will be able to keep up with math homework when it does become more demanding in later years. Do you know that one of the main reasons freshmen drop out of college is due to not being able to keep up with math? It's because they cannot handle the math homework load, and didn't build up the sheer stamina needed for college. Doing homework every single day, or at least five times a week (even if it is only for ten minutes, every day, to start with) can absolutely make the difference between succeeding and failing in college.

As an adult guiding your child, the task falls on your shoulders to make homework time a priority, a time for you and your child to be even playful together. By transforming homework time from a scary, frustrating, lonely time to a happy, fun family time, where you are together, sharing what you do know, turning the unknown into the newly learned, practicing, and playing together, you are guiding your child to become a lifelong joyful learner. You have the power to shape their learning process for life. This is a priceless gift.

When you combine being a role model, learning and sharing your life experiences, and owning your power to shape your child's learning process, your child *will* want to listen and follow your lead, regardless of your math level. Together you can ensure that your child's potential is maximized and this can truly be life-transforming. I'll let a few kids and their parents (both don't-care-about-math and love-math types) describe their experience using this process. This is what's possible when kids reconnect with the joy of learning and find themselves back on the road of becoming efficient learners:

> "My grade went from a D to an A within five weeks." —*a sixth grader*
>
> "From fifth grade on, I have always been terrible at math. Each year became harder for me. My lack of skills just kept on piling on each other all through school and high school. During my senior year, I decided to take PreCalculus/Trigonometry which soon turned into a bad idea within the first month. I had two tutors helping with my homework before, but it didn't help me. It's been two months; I received my first B+ on a test. Not only did my grades go up but also did my confidence. Fellow students in my class would now ask me about their homework!" *-an eleventh grader*
>
> "I don't like math so that didn't help our grandson…[working with Dr. Pan and the MAMMA process], our grandson gained confidence in school areas of his life…where I used to see discouragement in his life, he now has a desire for learning and the confidence to fall along the journey knowing that is it just part of learning." *-a grandfather of a sixth grader*

For many parents who want to help their kids with math, shifting from "doing math" to "developing MathAbility" is not intuitive at first. And over the years, I've come to understand that this is largely because we may have gotten used to gauging math success by the grades our kids achieve. But good math grades are just the by-product of an effective learning process.

Put it another way. Just like in an orchard, where the fruit is the end reward of tending to the water, soil, fertilizer, and sunlight, solid math grades are the natural results of kids mastering MathAbility. Very few kids can master math concepts *and* MathAbility without adults' help. The best part of separating teaching math concepts from building and managing MathAbility is *every* caring adult can teach MathAbility to a child regardless of their own math level. So, by tending to the *elements* that bring math success, good grades follow naturally.

One more insight about math grades when they're not ideal is this: just because a child's grades are not good, it doesn't mean their math is broken or that they can't do the math. But it does mean some aspect of their learning process is not supporting the weight of the math they are learning in school. By building and managing MathAbility, you're establishing a stronger learning process that will support the weight. So the way you can help is by looking outside of math concepts and re-evaluating what elements in your child's learning process are not up to par. With all the life experience and wisdom that *you have* already accumulated, you *can* teach MathAbility because it has everything to do with learning (which you've already mastered) and very little to do with math concepts (which most of us don't care for anyway).

In the next chapter, let's take a drive through the K–12 math landscape and look at each of the five distinct phases along the way, the pitfalls within each phase, and some fun opportunities as well. Once you know the landscape, I'll show you what sort of positive family interactions others have shared with their kids while building and managing MathAbility, and the extraordinary ways that parents like you have actively transformed their kids' relationship with math.

CHAPTER 7

What Kids Are Learning in K–12 Math, Pitfalls and Often-Missed Opportunities

> *The days are long, but the years are short.*
> *—Gretchen Rubin*

To familiarize kids and parents with the sequential nature of the K–12 math curriculum, I developed this math roadmap shortly after I started working on the MAMMA process in 2003. The five-phase progression across the K–12 math landscape[8] looks like this:

---

[8] © 2020 Door-2-Math. Designed by Dr. Feenix Pan; Illustrated by B. Jonquil.

LANDMARKS OF K-12 MATH AT A GLANCE

K - 3RD

Arithmetic 1
- Addition
- Subtraction
- Multiplication

3RD - 5TH

Arithmetic 2
- Long Division
- Decimals
- Percentages
- Fractions

6TH - 10TH

Pre-Algebra
- Order of Operations
- Variables
- Expressions
- Word Problems

Algebra 1
- Solve & Graph One-Variable Equations
- System of Equations
- Exponents
- Quadratic Equations

Geometry
- Parallel Lines & Angles
- Congruent & Similar Triangles
- Circles
- Surface Area & Volume

11TH - 12TH

Algebra 2
- Polynomials & Rational Functions
- Exponential & Logarithmic Functions
- Matrices & System of Equations
- Intro to Probability

Trigonometry & PreCalc
- Angular & Linear Velocities
- Laws of Sine and Cosine Functions
- Trig Identities
- Series & Sequences

12TH - COLLEGE

Advanced Mathematics
- Calculus I (req. for LAW schools)
- Calculus II (req. for MEDICAL schools)
- Calculus III (req. for ENGINEERING schools)

PHASE 1: K - 3RD GRADE - FUNDAMENTAL MATH
PHASE 2: 3RD - 5TH GRADE - FOUNDATIONAL MATH
PHASE 3: 6TH - 10TH GRADE - FUNCTIONAL MATH
PHASE 4: 11TH - 12TH GRADE - FORTRESS MATH
PHASE 5: 12TH GRADE/COLLEGE - FUN MATH

There is more than one destination. Not every kid wants or needs to get "over the mountain passes" of high math and pursue a career that depends on advanced calculus. There are lots of great destinations.

At the same time, no one wants to get stuck in a ditch, or lost in the desert. Not being able to master the basic foundations of mathematics leaves you stranded in a ditch. Never figuring out how to solve world problems is like running out of gasoline partway through the desert. Some kids lose their way in the hills of algebra or in the mountains of trigonometry, and some who aim to get over the mountain get stuck in the high passes of calculus. There's no shame in getting lost or stuck: everyone needs help to reach their goals. Teachers, tutors, volunteers, and classmates as well as family are all part of every kid's math "caravan."

Whenever a kid gets stuck, most parents like you experience confusion or heartache because you'll want to help but sometimes you won't know how. If you struggled with math yourself, or if you learned math one way and now it is being taught a different way, your most important work is to hang onto that wish to help. Don't let it turn into its opposite—a sense of frustration. *Even without understanding the math, you can help.* Stay with that wish. Parents who stay hopeful, optimistic, and encouraging are the roadside repair team.

Phase 1. The lowlands of K-third grade: FUNDAMENTAL MATH

The first phase is from kindergarten to third grade. In some families, this starts in preschool or at home with math play. This is **fundamental math** and is where a child's math journey begins. There is a very old saying: "Well begun is half done." This means children who start off with a good, solid understanding of math's foundations will be able to travel faster and farther before they encounter any problems. This is the phase where children learn counting, what numbers look like, and adding, subtracting, and multiplying. For most kids, subtraction is the hardest to learn. It can help to use other words like "take away" to explain subtraction. The hardest part of subtraction is this: it's the first time that sequence matters. When you add or multiply, you get the same correct answer however you start:

3 + 5 and 5 + 3 both get you to 8.

2 × 7 and 7 × 2 both get you 14.

That's not the case with subtraction:

3 − 5 is NOT the same as 5 − 3.

When it comes to subtraction, understanding the words suddenly matters much, much more. The best help a parent can give is practice, practice, practice, and developing verbal fluency with the math words. There are some very good picture books available at libraries to help families build math fluency.

My experience has been that Montessori schools are usually very good at this phase because they give kids many attractive options to engage with math. Kindergarten and first graders who get to hold objects to learn to count, add, subtract, and multiply do much better than kids who are only shown numbers on paper.

Another observation is that the more often children practice adding and subtracting and multiplying, the easier the next phase will be for them. What kids learn in this phase helps them "level up" for the next phase where they will be learning long division.

What are the pitfalls of this phase? The biggest pitfall is thinking and then telling kids "Oh, this isn't important" or "There is time to catch up later." That often is not true. The biggest pitfall for kids is trying to get by just by memorizing numbers on paper, like with flashcards. To stay on the math road kids need to do actual counting of objects. Give them things to count: pennies or crayons or buttons or small toys or dry beans from the kitchen, things you have around the house, especially things the child sees and uses. It makes math more real if you spend time together counting and adding beans, then put them in a pot and cook them for part of your supper. This is, after all, how math started: people counted the things that mattered to them.

Now, some of the fun facts for this phase. Your child's unique learning style will start to reveal itself, so keep an eye open for that. Do they like to hear your voice? Do they really want to touch and hold the things they count? Do they like seeing the numbers on paper and quickly figure out that these little symbols represent things, and ideas? Do they figure out patterns by themselves, or do they like to figure out patterns with you?

This phase really is the best time to develop a homework (more like home play) routine. Set aside space each day to do the math, and play with a child. Vigorously defend this together time. The time you spend learning how math works is a gift you give that will affect your child's entire life.

Lastly, sloppy writing of numbers can really trip any child up, so make sure that clear, readable writing is mastered in this phase. It's a simple thing, but you would be really surprised how many points kids can lose down the road if their numbers don't look right. Make sure that your child's 4s look like a 4 and doesn't look like a 7 or a 9. Also, 1s and 7s need to be clearly different. So do 3s and 5s.

Phase 2. The twists and bends of third–fifth grade: FOUNDATIONAL MATH

The second phase is between third grade and fifth grade. This is what we call the **foundational phase** of their math journey. Kids start learning long division, decimals, percentages, and fractions. The material covered in this phase is essential to lay the foundation for pre-algebra that's coming their way next. During this phase, kids need to be able to work with numbers on paper, because long division and decimals are hard to "show" in any other way. However, there are some good math tools and toys for showing fractions; and a great way to demonstrate basic percentages is with pennies, nickels, dimes, quarters, and dollars. Each penny is like one percent (1%) of a dollar; dimes are 10 percent of a dollar, and quarters are 25 percent of a dollar. Be sure to explain to your kid that the word "cent" comes from the Latin word for "hundred"; that's why there are 100 pennies or "cents" to a dollar, and 100 years to a century.

What you might not know for this phase is just how essential fractions will be in your child's math future. All math concepts from here onwards are going to be built on the concept of fractions. One more time: **All math concepts from here onwards are going to be built on the concept of fractions**. Mastering fractions is going to save you and your child tons of tears and headaches later on. You may be able to help your child by finding simple practice books that focus on fractions. Even if you don't like math, I encourage you to find a way to help your child understand fractions. It will be worth your effort. Pie circles, for example, are visual and fun. So are rectangles drawn on graph paper, and then coloring in different fractions of the rectangle. If you make a rectangle on graph paper with 12 squares, and color in 3 of the squares, you have just made the fraction 3/12. If you draw a shape on graph paper out of seven squares (it can be an odd-looking shape as long as all seven squares are chunked together) and color in 2 of them, you have just made the fraction 2/7.

It used to be that fractions were taught before percentages and decimals because decimals and percentages are just fractions based on using tens and hundreds as that number on the bottom, the "denominator." Most schools now teach decimals first because most calculators only show decimals. It takes specially programmed calculators to show fractions. However, there are times and circumstances when fractions are accurate, and decimals are only an approximate answer. This is *always* the case when round or curved shapes, like pipes or balls, are being measured. If we wish to live in a world where pipes that carry water, oil or gas fit right and don't break easily, we need engineers who know how to use fractions and radians (the math of round shapes) and do not rely on the approximate measurements of decimals.

The big pitfall for this phase is that kids are expected to shift, rather quickly, from simple math which can be done by adding, subtracting, and multiplying to concept-based mathematics. If they get a flat tire on the math road, they cannot understand new material. When schools' instructional programs take into account multiple intelligences and different learning styles, it is easier to cover this part of the road. Teachers who can show kids how to use Singapore Math[9] methods to set up and solve math problems can also help bridge the chasm that divides thinking about math in terms of objects you count to thinking about patterns and concepts in math.

Another pitfall I see at work is that you may not appreciate how critical fractions are at this phase, especially if your child begins to struggle for the first time with math. And if they are starting to give you a little bit of a hard time when it comes to homework, you might be tempted to let them off the hook hoping maybe next quarter or next semester things will get better. But, since math concepts build upon each other, your child may have missed something that their teacher in the next semester may assume they already know, which means their ability to understand math may go downhill from there. Your child's understanding of math will not improve without help. So I really encourage you to do whatever you can to help your child maintain good homework habits, and find ways to practice the math skills they are being shown in school.

This is also usually the time in a child's life where friendships become very important. Many parents find it can be a wonderful help to arrange study groups where classmates get together at each other's house or at a study place, help each other out, and enjoy a meal together.

This can be a great time to use pizza math to explore fractions. Let me give a small example: a pizza cut into 4 slices makes the fractions 1/4, 2/4, 3/4, and 4/4, with 4/4 being the whole pizza. (Any time the number on top is the same as the number on the bottom, you have a whole.) A pizza cut into 8 slices makes the fractions 1/8, 2/8, 3/8, 4/8, 5/8, 6/8, 7/8, and 8/8. Kids will very quickly notice that a 1/4 slice of pizza is like 2 of the 8-slice pizza. That is because, in math, 1/4 = 2/8. And if you have lots of pizzas sliced into eighths, a very hungry kid might eat 10 slices, or 10/8, which is more than a whole pizza. Any time the numerator is greater than

---

[9] The Singapore Math method is focused on mastery achieved through intentional sequencing of concepts. Instead of pushing through rote memorization, students are guided to learn to think mathematically and rely on the depth of knowledge gained in previous lessons.

the denominator, you have more than one whole and a hungry kid eats more than one whole pizza.

Here is another tip: if for some reason your math experience has not been a totally positive one, do your best to not make your math become your kids' problem. If you talk about math in a disparaging way, or sigh heavily or say math doesn't matter, you might be putting water in their gas tank or letting the air out of their tires just when they need all the momentum they can get.

Here are some fun facts for this phase. This is a really great age to let your children teach you something. Give them the opportunity to share, such as counting money together to practice fractions and decimals, or perhaps baking together, or doing pizza fractions. Look for opportunities to become a partner with your child and learn along with them.

Phase 3. The hills of algebra in sixth–tenth grade: FUNCTIONAL MATH

Let's move to phase three. This is a big one. It covers from sixth grade to about tenth grade, so basically three years of middle school, which will mostly be pre-algebra, and two years of high school. For most high schoolers, this means Algebra I and Geometry. If your kids like math, this will probably be the phase where they will outstrip you, if they haven't done so already. You'll need to find a way to be okay with this and find different ways to stay connected with them when it comes to math. Remember, even just providing the structure and support of regular homework habits, encouragement, and good meals will be a tremendous help.

This is the **functional phase** of their math journey. I call this functional math because this is the math we use for everyday life. This is the math that will help you get along and not be left behind or taken advantage of in everyday life. We use the math covered in this functional phase to buy groceries, by estimating how much things will cost, including tax; to pay our bills and balance a budget; to solve problems; to make measurements for home improvements; to buy houses and pay mortgages; to buy a car, get a loan, deal with credit cards, interest rates, and so on. So this is quite an important phase. This is also the sort of math that people used to learn "on the job" by helping build stuff in the family workshop or by working in the family store or restaurant. It is easier for most children to learn math if they can do some of the things the math represents. Instead of sending your kid off to play while you pay the bills or estimate a grocery list, or measure the room and figure out where the new couch or TV will go, involve them in the process. Yes, it will slow you down, but this is about helping them learn, not about getting the task done as quickly as possible.

Getting through the hills of pre-algebra means being able to navigate the slow curves, the gear shifts, and speed changes of new math skills. It also means enjoying the views. Some kids will discover they love being able to estimate quickly how much things will cost, especially if they are faster and better at it than their parents. (Be happy for them when they are, and congratulate them.) They will learn how to compare prices and find the best bargains, how to estimate sale discounts and the extra cost of taxes, how to plan out a project, and how to use math in all sorts of real-world ways. In math class, good grades will depend on more than math smarts; they'll need good math habits to avoid running out of gas or taking a wrong turn and getting lost. Some of these essential math skills and habits include:

- Being able to estimate the correct answer before doing the computations.

- Checking how closely your estimate matches the answer.

- Writing out a sentence with a blank space for the answer to a word problem.

- Including the units of the answer. This is so important as more than one multibillion-dollar engineering project has failed when team members lost track of the units.

- Showing all your work, and showing it neatly.

In pre-algebra, word problems become increasingly complex and realistic. Kids who excel at these sorts of problems are on track for careers in science, engineering, finance, and even medicine. Good reading comprehension skills will help keep kids on the road because they can read the road signs. If they haven't already, a child needs to start developing good test-taking skills.

If you do have a child who happens to be struggling with Algebra I, don't panic. It's not the end of the world. Even older kids' math skills can be turned around. If your kid is struggling in this phase, I really encourage you not to focus on the grades, because doing so just gets frustrating for everyone. Instead, you really want to dig in and find the root cause. Often it is the fraction or some other key concept in the previous phase that didn't get explained well or that they didn't understand.

Now let me give you a little insight into the pitfalls regarding this phase. In a perfect world, Algebra I and Algebra II should be taken back to back, and followed by Geometry. But our education system is not set up like this. Instead, most kids end up taking Algebra I and then Geometry for a whole year, before circling back to Algebra II. This is because of the PSAT, SAT, and ACT scheduled tests. This is not ideal. Let me explain why. Algebra II is really a continuation of Algebra I, and a whole year of Geometry in between is just too big of a break and a gap in math continuity for most kids. For this reason, Algebra II has often been dubbed the "crash and burn" class of high school math.

The smart thing to do is to really prepare for it the summer before your child gets to Algebra II classes. This is why, for this phase, I typically recommend that you look ahead a little bit after your child finishes the Geometry class. Maybe take an online class with Khan Academy (a free online course), find an equivalent course through a local community college summer program, or consider tutoring or an educational support group. If you have a more ambitious kid who is oriented toward a science major, take an Algebra II class at the community college in the summer, ahead of the high school schedule. Then the high school class becomes a review. I know this is a bit more effort, but I promise you it's so worth the effort. It'll avoid the crash and burn, protect the high school GPA, and set your child up far ahead.

Another thing that's helpful to know is that as early as ninth grade, certainly by tenth grade, academic grades become vital for building a strong college application. This is because colleges use these grades to evaluate applicants. Solid grades during high school years count, and they count a lot.

Some fun facts about this phase. This is the age where kids can potentially latch on to a lifelong passion. And at this age, kids love to start imagining their future, and even visit colleges. Go with their enthusiasm. Look for new ways to expose them to new topics and career opportunities and discuss with them how math will play a part in whatever they like best.

Phase 4. Mountains of Algebra II and Trig/PreCalculus in eleventh and twelfth grade: FORTRESS MATH

Let's move to the fourth phase, which I call **fortress math**. Most kids who finished Geometry in tenth grade will be taking Algebra II in eleventh grade and Trigonometry/PreCalculus in twelfth grade. (Some schools divide Algebra classes into Algebra 1, 2, and 3.) If a child's math is advanced, then the track is Geometry in ninth grade, Algebra II in tenth grade, and Trig/Pre-Calculus in eleventh grade. Some schools offer AP courses with even more advanced options, including Calculus and Physics, while others offer applied mathematics classes for kids who wish to strengthen their basic and practical math abilities.

One common pitfall in this phase is that kids give up on math too early (especially Algebra II). Because this phase is a critical transition phase into the upcoming Calculus or Statistics, what kids do in this phase matters a lot. I'm not saying we want to force them into taking calculus classes, but it is very important that all kids keep their options open and their math skills active. And if they are to get careers in fields like physics, biology, economics, dynamic systems, chemistry, pharmacy, or engineering, they need to pass calculus.

One of the best ways to avoid the pitfalls is to help your child do some review math of Algebra I and II every day, or practice geometry problem solving. Keep on encouraging them to do practical math at home: paying bills together, estimating the cost of groceries and clothes and taxes, checking receipts to make sure there were no mistaken extra charges, adding up household expenses in a ledger, balancing a checking or savings account, measuring the sizes of rooms, and making maps of your home or neighborhood.

Phase 5. High passes of advanced calculus/statistics in twelfth grade and college: FUN MATH

Moving into the last phase, which is the fifth phase, is really FUN. What I'll focus on here is the popular calculus family, which has three courses, namely Calculus I, Calculus II, and Calculus III. At the high school level, they're somewhat abbreviated and combined into just two courses: Calculus AB and Calculus BC. If your kid got here, congratulations. They really deserve a big pat on the back.

I call this **fun math** because all those seemingly random things that had to be memorized before start to make sense and fall into place here. Take, for example, the volume of a sphere. My high school calculus teacher got me hooked on math in this phase. I still remember that one day he took a basketball, drilled a hole into it, and then filled the ball with water. And he told us that we learn calculus so we can calculate the volume of how much water he put in there. "And you can even calculate how long it is going to take them to drain this whole basketball," he promised. The class did the calculation and the measured data was right on. Learning calculus is like suddenly discovering what those gears in a car are for: the really steep inclines. And if the vistas in the hills were great, the views from the mountains are *spectacular*.

One thing I really want you to know about this phase is that high school calculus and college calculus are *not* the same. College-level calculus is taught faster, more in-depth, and has stiffer competition. And Calculus II is actually the hardest of the calculus family. So try to avoid the trap of going from Calculus I in high school to Calculus II in college. Most colleges and universities understand that this can be a problem and they will administer a math entrance exam. Based on a kid's grade on this exam, the college will recommend which college math class to take first. Please do not get upset if your son or daughter is told to take Calculus I over again, or even college Algebra II. Be ready to tell your son or daughter that sometimes it is better to start college doing the math you already know—or will easily remember—to protect their college GPA and give themselves time to get adjusted to college schedules, heavy loads of homework, and other new experiences.

One more thing before we wrap up this phase: senioritis. Your kid might be asking, "Oh, another level of math in my senior year?" And you might be thinking too: If my kid already has enough math credits to graduate, wouldn't it be easier to just let them coast and not take another advanced class? This is the common pitfall of senioritis. On one hand, they worked so hard to get here and it's tempting to just coast along. On the other hand, this is the last phase where you, as the parent, can encourage your child to take a little bit of risk while they still have your support close by. From my personal experience, I love encouraging kids around me to push on and take a little bit of risk while they're still at home, and still in high school. The reason I can say this with confidence is that most kids apply to colleges in eleventh grade or the very beginning of twelfth grade before senior year grades are part of their transcript. So taking a challenging or "risky" math class won't hurt their college application process.

Make your own roadmap

If you are reading this book because you have kids in your life who are on the math journey, you may wish to sit down together and identify where on the road you and your child are right now. Where have they had any math car trouble on the road? Have there been rough patches where the road may need to be patched or repaved? Do they have a destination in mind? Are you both willing to see how far along the math road your child can travel? Does having a math roadmap affect how your child views math homework? With older kids, does it affect your choices of universities and colleges?

In the next chapter, I'll show you some math journeys other families have gone through. I want to show you the sort of ways other families have built solid math memories with their kids.

CHAPTER 8

Smiles: Successful Math Journeys as Other Families Lived Them

> *If equal affection cannot be*
> *Let the more loving one be me.*
> *—W.H. Auden*

Here are what positive interactions and joyful results can look like. Most of these examples are from my experiences with our own two kids, and many other responses in italics are gathered by my friend[10] from families that I had the privilege of interacting with while they helped their kids build and manage MathAbility. I'm using a question and answer format here to best capture what parents had to say. As you read these, ask yourself: What methods and specific activities do I see others using to build the four core skills of MathAbility that will help my child with their organizational skills, critical thinking skills, test-taking skills, and ability to formulate clear and effective questions?

---

[10] Christina Wozney gathered most of the other parents' feedback for this chapter.

Question #1: What are some of the ways your kids showed enjoyment of math from an early age?

What parents say:

> "We had a Montessori preschool in our neighborhood. Our two-year-old loved counting and sorting shapes."
>
> "Train sets. I am sure our kids got an early sense of math by assembling train sets and pushing those magnetic train cars around the tracks. Maybe it made all those distance-traveled word problems easier to understand later on."
>
> "Right from first grade, our son loved to talk about and show us what he learned in math class."
>
> "Ironically, when our oldest child was little, I was doing my own math homework. So I would give him problems to solve: $1 + x = 2$. What is x? And that's how it started."

Here is my experience:

Our son showed interest by counting rice balls on his plate before he could walk. One day I saw him rolling his rice balls from one plate to another, over and over again. I knew he was counting but had no words for what he was doing. I showed him three fingers on my hand, and when he looked up, I then rolled three rice balls onto a plate and said, "Three," and he repeated, "Three." And on we went.

Our daughter came to math more slowly. One summer, when she was about three or four years old, we left her with my parents while we went to see a movie. Afterward, when we came back to pick her up, she showed me how she could count on her fingers and toes to add two numbers

Question #2: What were some games or activities that incorporated math?

What parents say:

> "We played a ton of Monopoly. Great math game. Money and dice. Correct change. At first, our youngest child had to count all the dots on the dice, every time. One day, I pointed to one of the dice and asked, 'How many dots is that?' And she answered, without counting, 'Four.'"
>
> "My child loves to measure things around the house with a tape measure."
>
> "The school had a sewing class. Our daughter learned to make toys and clothes."

Here is my experience:

The kitchen is a perfect place to incorporate math. Take baking, for example; it requires measuring liquid, solids, and often counting eggs, not to mention setting oven temperatures and a timer. And then there's cutting the cake: That's doing fractions, isn't it? We picked up an old table scale, the kind that chemists use in their labs, and our kids had a fun time weighing things in the kitchen. I wanted them to experience math, touch math, and interact with math because math is all around us.

Another thing I did was have them figure out what the change would be when we were in the grocery checkout line. I'd give them a dollar or two in coins and have them first add up the coins, then buy something. They got to keep the change if they gave the right "guesstimate" of the amount of money they'd have left after their purchase.

When they got older, I'd have them help with the entire shopping list and asked them to give me their estimates for how much all the grocery items in the shopping cart would cost. Since they put all sorts of stuff in the cart, from fruit roll-ups to toys for our dogs, at the checkout line I took all the goodies out and told them that, if they could estimate the total cost of the groceries, then I'd be willing to pay for whatever they had picked out. At first, they were way off. So I never had to say "No" to their impulse desires. I got away with that for the longest time. But then our daughter got smart. She started to pay attention to the cost of the items being put into the cart. And then she got good at rounding the cost off to the nearest dollar and using mental math to add. (NO calculator. That was part of the deal.) She turned the table on me. When she got really good at estimating, I had to eat my words. She started to hunt out the most expensive ice cream and pick her favorite flavors.

Question #3: What were some ways that your child demonstrated a preferred learning style?

What parents say:

> *"Our daughter loves music; she was memorizing songs at a very young age. In school, she learns Spanish more easily through songs than any other way. She loves the Schoolhouse Rock and Tim Griffin CDs, and another one called Nature Nut. If it rhymes or is set to music, she can remember it better."*

> *"If our boy can see it in a picture, he can usually figure it out. He likes geometry best of all because the diagrams practically show him the answer. But he gets into trouble if the picture is not drawn right. Then he has to make his own drawing."*

Here is my experience:

Our daughter was a strong auditory learner. Picture books and story time were her things. She preferred to read her math problems out loud. So when she started violin lessons, I turned digits of the irrational number pi into song lyrics to "Mary Had a Little Lamb." It went like this: 3.141592 653 589 793238 462643.

Our son was more of a kinesthetic learner. He wanted to physically touch the objects of his interest, be they Lego pieces, puzzles, or action figures. Puzzles, by the way, are a fantastic way for kinesthetic kids and visual kids to learn.

Question #4: How did you use math around the home or during the day, and how did you include your child?

What parents say:

> "We counted everything. And we read directions together. I'd ask questions to see if they understood, and let them ask me questions."
>
> "On the playground, pushing them on the swings, I'd count to one hundred as I pushed. They loved that. Soon they started counting along."
>
> "In the kitchen, measuring ingredients for pancakes. We have an ounce and metric measuring cups, so we'd compare how the same amount of water or milk is measured in the two different measurement systems."

Here is my experience:

Other than teaching it, I use math around our home mostly with time. I find clocks fascinating, especially those round analog clocks because they contain difficult math; they don't use units that add up to hundred, instead, they use units that add up to 60. And there's a lot of history behind analog clocks too. I bring up the clock at work also because it is a fantastic way for kids, especially visual learners, to start getting used to learning math and multiplication.

I tried to share my awareness of math in daily life with my kids. When we drove together, I told them to open the window and feel the difference between 45 mph when we were in the car and 15 mph near the school zone. When they got older, we looked at the speedometer because they asked about why there are two sets of numbers. "One is for the metric system," I told them. Then we looked up why the US is one of the few remaining countries still using the English system (but not England, go figure).

Another fun thing we did a lot when I was driving them around was at gas stations. Those were wonderful places where they could earn spending money. After they filled the gas up, they could earn a percentage of the money we spent at the pump. If they could figure what five percent of the $21 that I spent at the pump, they could get $1.20! And if they were up to it, they could keep the change if they went inside the gas station and figured out how much a pack of gum was with tax.

I tried to relate math and numbers and the cost of goods for them early on. When my son became fascinated with those one-minute hourglasses, I had him figure out the number of seconds in a day (the answer is 86,400 seconds) and later on when our daughter got interested in the Rubik's cube, we took one apart and put it back together. We looked up those fascinating things. By the way, a fun fact we found: because a $2 \times 2 \times 2$ Rubik cube has 3,674,160 combinations, if you fiddle with this $2 \times 2 \times 2$ cube randomly for eight continuous hours a day, you will solve it by pure chance roughly two or three times per year.

Question #5: What were the best math teachers like? And what do you do with the ones that are not so good?

What parents and kids say:

> "My own favorite math teacher was funny, yet also strict. He set very clear rules for the class, and he treated everybody fairly. He was also the football coach, so the boys in the class had a lot of respect for him."

> "Prepared. She had lesson plans that accommodate students at different levels and with different learning styles, and she had extra worksheets and game options for kids who finished their work early."

> "My musical daughter had a terrible experience in ninth grade. It was the first time math was hard for her. The teacher was everybody else's favorite math teacher, but she couldn't understand him. She said she felt like Charlie Brown: all she heard was 'Wah wah, wah wah....' She failed Algebra II when all her classmates said it was the best math class ever. When she repeated Algebra II with a different teacher, the difference was like night and day. She said she liked the sound of his voice, so she could follow his explanations. He was very patient and kind, and he worked with students after class if they were stuck."

Here is my experience:

Good math teachers are like water, guiding, and carrying their students' learning canoes to the final destination with ease and grace. They don't rush their students' learning.

One time, I was volunteering at our kids' middle school class. The teacher was covering percentages that day. She asked the class, "So, what is a 10 percent tip for a $20 breakfast?" (Which, by the way, is a meager $2 tip). A young girl, whom I'll call Britney, raised her hand. "Yes, Britney? What's your answer and tell us how you got it."

Britney said: "I always leave a $20 tip for a $20 breakfast. That's 10 percent, right?"

I remember thinking, "Um, that's a 100 percent tip!" (I waitressed my way through most of my college years, and how I wished for that kind of *amazing* tip.) At the same time, I felt for this young teacher and wondered what she would do. Some teachers would ignore the wrong answer, others would lecture the class, using Britney's answer as an example of bad math. But this young teacher did none of that. Instead, she said, "Awesome try, Britney!" Then she held up her hand to forestall the kids who were waving their hands, anxious to correct their classmate, and said, "So, if the service was excellent, would you double your tip?" Beaming with pride, young Britney said, "My mom was a waitress and she said it's a hard job!" One by one, those impatient waving hands dropped down as the teacher showed the young kid how to shift one decimal point to the left to create a 10 percent tip (from $20.00 to $2.00). The teacher understood that there was more than one lesson here: there was the percentage math, and there was the example of Britney having a kind and generous heart.

One of the best things I did for my kids was train them to understand that all teachers are not the same, and to expect to have both good and so-so teachers as part of their life at school. While most teachers want to help, not all of them understand what kids are actually asking.

So early on, I taught my kids how to formulate effective questions to the teacher using **six words in a sequence** formula. The six words are in bold font below:

"Teacher, **I know** [X] **but I need** [Y] **because** [Z]."

For example, my son who was learning pre-algebra at the time would say: "I know [we're solving for a variable], but I need [to see how you solved it one more time] because [the last two steps were not quite clear to me]. Be very specific. We also practiced this formula when they made requests at home. My daughter would say "Mom, I know [you want me to do all my school work in one sitting], but I need [to break it up a little] because [it helps me to 'not zone out']."

Just like parenting, teaching is often a thankless job. Unless we are willing to pay them the respect they deserve and compensate them for what their job is really worth, I'd say investing what little precious energy we have on helping our kids ask more effective questions is helpful to teachers, and is one way to mitigate their low compensation.

Question #6: What are some ways teachers helped your child flourish and succeed with math?

What parents and kids say:

> "My child's teacher sat down with my child every day in zero-hour for a month to get him caught up."

> "Our daughter said her math teacher showed her how algebra could be handled with blocks, not just numbers and letters. Made so much sense."

> "Our child struggled with algebra until her teacher brought the Algebra Lab and online visual learning tools."

> "My son's favorite teacher never rushed through a problem. He was very patient, and he let students tell him what the next step needed to be, even when they were wrong, and then they'd have to go back and find the mistake and fix it. The teacher said that was good practice for life, and he'd ask, 'Were there any ways to know that was not the right step to take?'"

> "My son's favorite tutor listened to him, and let him explain where his understanding of math ran out. She helped him find patterns in multiplication so that suddenly he was able to memorize—and understand—multiplication for the first time."

"This seems like a small thing, but it made such a difference for our daughter. Her geometry teacher took the time to make sure every single student could use the compass and protractor and other tools correctly. This meant she could measure angles and lines and get correct answers, and so could her classmates, and they could compare results."

"I didn't realize this until our son was in junior high, but he needed to be able to reason his way through a math concept; he was very logical. It wasn't enough to say, 'This works, do it this way.' When he had a math teacher who asked him to explain his reasoning, and who showed him the logic behind the math, he began to enjoy math again."

"My favorite math teacher took fifteen minutes at the beginning of almost every class to go through homework problems that had stumped us the night before. We told him the problem we couldn't solve, and then we solved them together as a class. Only then would he move on to new material."

"Our teacher told us how he'd used math in his other jobs before teaching, and he made us solve real-world problems, like how much it costs to pay for a year's worth of diapers, or how taxes diminished your take-home pay but were used for things like roads and street lights and hospitals, things we all used. I liked that he put bonus questions on every quiz and test so we could bring our grades up."

"My Algebra teacher always gave us plenty of examples of how any algebra rules worked with actual numbers. I never understood an algebra pattern until I saw it worked out with numbers about five or six times. He shows us three or four examples in class, then we'd practice some more for homework. He'd usually include an extra tricky one as a bonus challenge. The smart kids usually figured them out. I didn't, but once I saw it worked out on the board in class the next day, I usually understood the trick, and I'd remember it when one just like it was on the test."

Some of my favorite responses are from my own colleagues:

"I try to be kind and clear with my students, I give them clear guidelines on what will be covered on the test and do my best to stick to that guideline when I make up the test."

"I engage my students with shortcuts and tricks. Once I made up a trick multiplication question on the board. I wrote out 18 three-digit numbers, and at the last second, I put a zero in. As you know, everything multiplied by zero is zero. They went wild with that!"

"I want kids to feel confident in their own ability, so I tend to give a lot of repetitive work before moving onto the next concept. With confidence everything is possible."

"Movement and musicality are important tools in learning and succeeding with math, so in my class, we sing a lot of equations together."

Here is my own experience:

When I struggled with math early on, my teacher taught me how to think critically. He turned my failure, ignorance, despair, and self-doubt into, "Oh, I can see my way through now." He taught me how to fill the gap between what I tried to do and what needed to be done to solve a problem.

When I went to him for help with a homework problem, he kept asking me, "Now, what were you trying to do here?" I tried my best to explain to him what I was trying to do. After he listened for a while, he'd say, "Well, if that's what you're trying to do, isn't the next logical step this?" After a while, I started to reason myself forward, just as he did. When I made mistakes, I was able to detect the error in my way of thinking and find a different path to correctly solve the problem.

Now let me also give you a negative space example, because while a good, kind, caring, and patient teacher is almost always best, the fact is, a bad, rude, or incompetent teacher can also be a learning experience—if you pay attention. I would even go as far as to say that when a "bad" teacher shows up, it's your chance as parents to really strengthen your child's character and bond with your child, but only if you stay in touch with your child and see the situation as an opportunity. Here's an example. When our daughter got to her sophomore year in high school, her teacher was a retired engineer who didn't bother to give lectures. "Read your own %$#@ textbook" was his way of toughening them up. I watched as my daughter first tried to argue with her teacher, then gathered some of her classmates to try to change the teacher, and when that didn't work, they all went to the principal to complain, and finally, they found a YouTube channel to teach themselves. They formed a study group to teach and quiz each other.

My daughter aced the class and so did everyone in her study group. Just as importantly, they learned that they could solve a real-world problem together, even when adults in positions of authority were unable or refused to handle the problem.

Question #7: What were the transitional times when math became harder?

So parents, let me ask you first: When did math become difficult for your child? Was it in transitioning from adding objects to adding numbers? From addition to multiplication? Multiplication to long division? Fractions to percentages? Or was it word problems? Or algebra, when suddenly x can mean three different things: either to multiply, or an unknown number you have to solve for, or a variable—which means it can have many values. That stumps a lot of kids right there, and they demand to know, not unreasonably, why there isn't a symbol that means "multiply now" that doesn't look like a letter, and let x be used only for an unknown, and use v when there is a variable? These are very good questions! Some textbooks and teachers do start to use a floating dot instead of x to indicate multiplication.

Here is my experience:

Math became hard for my daughter when she had to transition from addition to multiplication. She kept on using addition to figure out, say 6 × 7. She'd add six 7's together—slow and painful for me to watch, but she always got the right answer. I hoped there was something that would wake her up because adding is a poor man's way to multiply.

So this happened one day: We went to the grocery store and she wanted to buy bags of candies for a friend's Halloween party. Sensing a chance to ease her math transition, I asked how much I had to pay if each huge bag of M&Ms was $6 and she wanted seven bags, one for each of her friends. I told her she would have to figure it out before we got to the cashier. She told me flat-out that she'd have to go back to the classroom because the multiplication chart was on the classroom wall! I said, "Well, you can add the way you normally do." So, there she was, holding up the register line, and let me share this with you, adding a lot of numbers takes forever when others behind you are watching and waiting and wanting to get their own turn at the register. She finally got there: $42 dollars. I was glad to pay because that night she asked to see the shortcut to multiplication that I'd worked out with her brother. Don't you agree that motivation to learn and grow finds us at odd places?

Question #8: Did your kids need help developing or maintaining a work ethic for math homework? What helped?

What parents say:

"Study groups helped, being around smarter kids."

"It helped our son to have a long and serious talk with a school mentor he respected, about what kinds of math he needed for the career he wanted. He then realized the road he was on didn't lead to the destination he dreamed of and he would need to change his behaviors to aim himself towards his goals. He was told he had a real choice: change his behaviors and start doing his homework, or change his goals. He chose to change himself."

"Our daughter is very competitive. She wanted to be the best in at least some of her classes. When she figured out that she already had an edge in math, she concentrated on increasing her lead, by devoting a lot of energy and time to her math homework. What she started to do out of a competitive spirit turned into good habits."

"Getting good feedback and support, either from teachers or from us at home was helpful. We increased the allowance when homework started taking more time, and we'd take our kids out for pizza after they completed a big project."

Here is my experience:

While I was doing research for this book, it turned out that conscientiousness is a steady predictor not only for academic success, but for every kind of success in life, including happiness and good relationships.[11]

As mentioned earlier in this book, there's a Chinese saying: "How you do one thing is how you do everything." Having a work ethic matters when work is no longer fun or easy. But different kids come with different strengths and degrees of work ethic. Our daughter seemed to be born with a strong work ethic. When she got her clean laundry from the dryer, she dove in, sorting piece by piece and putting them all away. No fuss, no mess. And she did her math homework the same way, after the stubborn multiplication table incident. I almost feel that she was programmed in the womb with a strong work ethic. Now our son is a different story. He needed help. Tons of it.

I did a lot of things wrong when I first tried to develop a work ethic with my son. I got into my "I'll wear you down" mode; I nagged him to clean up this, pick up that. I made to-do lists for him and put them on the fridge, on his placemats, or bathroom mirrors; you name it, I tried it. This approach, I now know, works for some kids, but more often than not it only produces a short-term behavioral change. I was getting more and more frustrated, and our son got more and more resistant. What I didn't know was that he needed a lot of patient role modeling. I was brought up to believe we succeed only by being persistent. So whenever I gave up in frustration I felt like a quitter and the fear of failing as a mom was demoralizing.

But what I had going for me was that I was in contact with many child-centered families and many smart and experienced educators. To help their own kids achieve their full potential, they understood the importance of work ethic from very early on, and they explained to me that I was trying to win a battle *against* my son, and by doing so I was turning our relationship

---

[11] S. Roccas et al., "The Big Five Personality Factors and Personal Values", June 2002 Personality and Social Psychology Bulletin 28(6):789-801.

into a war. Those people showed me a different way of approaching how to develop a sense of work ethic. I got a lot of advice, tips, and resources.

One particular approach made all the difference. One mom's idea was to use putting away laundry together to role model work ethic. This was particularly appropriate for me because, at that time, laundry was the top issue. I'd been trying to force our son to put the laundry away. I would wash laundry and dump a pile of his things on his bed for him to put away. One time he fell off the bed because he'd gone to sleep on that big pile instead of putting the laundry away. After that, I put the laundry on the floor so at least he wouldn't fall off the bed and hurt himself. And there the laundry would stay, on the floor in a big pile.

After getting advice, instead of expecting him to do something and trying to force him to do it, laundry became something we did together. Now I understood that it was my responsibility and my work to be a role model, to show him how to do something properly, with love and patience.

Laundry was the best possible choice because putting laundry away is actually something I enjoy doing. I love folding laundry, and there was no way my son could ruin my joy, no matter what he said or how he behaved. And I knew I would have to be patient because even if I wasn't making a war of it anymore, it would still feel like a war zone to my son. Our relationship was damaged, and it needed to heal. So, for a month I put his laundry on the floor in his room, then without asking him to do anything, I would start sorting and folding and putting things away, enjoying the process, and he would sit there and watch me.

The mom who'd advised me had also told me, "You cannot react to his reaction. It's not about him, because he has to process how to get through a frustrating thing." And oh yes, he tried to push my buttons and get me upset. But I wouldn't have a fit, and that is the secret: pick something you enjoy; if you choose to go this route, demonstrate not just the skills it takes to accomplish the chore but also the joy you find in doing it well. My son hated laundry so much he couldn't fathom how I could not hate it. And of course, he hadn't paid attention, so he didn't really know how to put away the laundry.

For weeks he watched me from start to finish, finally seeing the actual process, and the skills involved in doing our laundry and putting it away. After weeks and months of just demonstrating and not reacting whenever he pushed my buttons, something magical happened. He started asking if he could help. I would ask him where to put the socks, or where would he like to have the shirts hung up. Little by little, he started participating with me and asking questions here and there. One day we just dumped the clothes on the floor and he jumped on the pile, still warm from the dryer, and asked, "Mom, can I do this all by myself this time?"

I remember thinking, "Why doesn't someone write a book about how to teach work ethic using everyday activities?" I was very aware that my old way of nagging had wasted a lot of time and energy, and how it had left me exhausted. I wish I had learned the lessons sooner.

Maintaining a work ethic isn't challenging. It's like riding a bicycle— once we experience the balance of the wheels, our body knows how to reproduce that experience over and over. And while getting up steep slopes is hard work, we know it is building our leg muscles. A strong and steady work ethic gets us up and over all sorts of hills in life. And just as we feel better with strong legs, we really do feel better when we have a deeply rooted work ethic.

Question #9: Were there times when you couldn't help with math homework? Why? How did you get past that?

What parents say:

"Our oldest son mentored his brothers and sister when math got hard for them and we didn't understand the math ourselves."

"Our problem was that the homework had to be done in the way the teacher showed. We both knew how to get the correct answer, but not in the way the teacher wanted! So our help was worse than no help at all, it just confused

> *our child. Another classmate had to practice the homework problems with our child. The lesson for all of us was when you need help, it isn't enough to find people who want to help. You need to find people who can help."*

Here's my experience:

It's inevitable that our kids' search for knowledge outgrows our ability to help. Instead of dreading it, calmly say three magic words: "I don't know." This phrase is magical because it frees us to join our kids in the search for answers.

One mom shared her story with me. One day her sixth grader asked about a word problem with decimals. The mom didn't know how to help because decimals were precisely where she'd gotten stuck in math years ago.

"But I was determined not to let my past affect my child's future," she told me.

"So what did you do?" I asked. I really wanted to know, because her daughter was acing everything I put in front of her for her accelerated tutoring, all the way to vector calculus.

"I'll tell you what I did. I pulled out my old photo album." She opened the one she was carrying. "I wanted to show it to you," she said.

Inside this old, faded album, some of the photos had turned yellow. She stopped at a page with two photos, both wrinkled at the corners.

"I told my girl that those two women weren't *allowed* to go to school. They had to pick cotton until their hands bled. After they were bone-tired, they still had to mend socks to keep food on the table. Then I told my baby girl to learn how to do that math, and then teach me. I told her, 'I really want to learn those decimals!'"

Question #10: What was their attitude towards taking tests?

What kids say:

"I would get so scared before a test that my brain would white out—nothing but static. I'd be unable to remember anything I'd studied. Eventually, I just got numb. I knew I'd fail another test. Then I took a class on how to take math tests that was offered at the local community college, and that helped."

"I hated tests. I knew I was able to solve the problems because I did them for homework. But something about that test paper...."

"I was one of those kids that liked taking tests. I saw them as a challenge and a game played between me and whoever wrote the test. I'd get excited in a way that made my mind clearer, more focused. I knew I had to read each question carefully, and the directions. Sometimes there are clues in directions. Then it was just a matter of finding the key to each problem. I wish life were as simple as tests."

"I used to get so anxious before a test. Then one day I realized: This doesn't help. Getting anxious doesn't make me better at math, it makes me feel worse. So I stopped worrying before tests, and I stopped worrying after tests. I still studied, but I made sure to get a good night's sleep instead of staying up late studying, and I pretended it was just another homework assignment. And my grades actually got better."

"This wasn't in math, but it changed my life. I was failing my first college science class and the teacher's assistant [T.A.] noticed. She asked how it was that I could ace all the homework and class assignments and then get low scores on tests. I said I didn't know. Then she asked me some test questions—questions I'd left blank on the last test—and I was able to answer them. She asked me if it was easier to answer questions I heard or questions I read. I told her I wanted to hear the questions. At home, I would say the homework out loud, but you're not allowed to talk during tests. The T.A. spoke to the instructor and got permission for me to take my final exam privately as a spoken test, not a written test. And I passed."

Here is my experience:

At first, tests didn't bother our daughter much. She treated them as if they were just another homework assignment. But that changed once tests got harder. The first time my daughter got a bad grade on a test I knew that unless she got help to overcome that fear of failing, it would be hard for her to recover the joy of learning. I see this at work often. Many kids come in without ever having had their "broken math noses" reset, and years later, they are still terrified of taking math tests. What we did for our daughter was to go out and celebrate her first failed test with her favorite ice cream at the mall. We associated something hard (failing a test) with something positive (a trip to the mall for her favorite ice cream) so there'd be less chance that test anxiety would grip and imprison her desire to learn. If you're worried this could encourage more bad grades down the road, you're not alone. But most kids would rather not fail, not even for ice cream. If a kid tries to be clever in *that* way, say it is a one-time deal, then figure out together what they need to have a better experience with the next test by looking closely at where they missed the mark on the last few tests. In a child's math journey, failing *one* math test is not a big deal in the long run, but not being able to recover from it is.

Our son never cared too much about tests. He was nonchalant about them. To him, it seemed that testing was an adults' game, one he didn't buy into one way or another. As he got older, he made a point to study after each class session, so he wouldn't have to cram for tests the night before.

Question #11: How did you help your child prepare for tests?

What parents say:

> "One of our three boys had test anxiety. We discussed preparation, confidence, and made an agreement that when a test was over, not to fret."
>
> "This may sound weird, but it was important. Our daughter has a gluten sensitivity, and it affects her mental clarity. We knew this because we'd had her tested for celiac disease, and we'd tracked her reactions to what she ate for

months. She literally 'eats stupid for breakfast' if she eats wheat products. When the AIMS tests were only two weeks away, she decided on her own to forego gluten foods until after the tests. She passed them all the first try—then went back to eating the bagels she loved."

Here is my experience:

The best way to prepare for tests is not to prepare for a test but instead understand the material. Parents who understand this pay attention to their child's study habits. If you have good homework habits, the test is like another homework assignment.

I help my clients focus on their self-knowledge when we prepare for a test. We discuss what they expect will be on the test, based on what the teacher told them in class. Then we assess if they have the concepts and skills to solve the kinds of problems they expect to see. To take their focus off the test scores, I ask of them before they take the test to predict how well they think they're going to do. If the actual score is within three points of that prediction I say "good job," because they've learned how to self-gauge. I show them I care about how well they know themselves more than I care about the grade itself.

Also, you might think success on a test is about knowing math, but there is a technique that's outside of math concepts that can help your child immediately. Here is the strategy I use to train my clients about test-taking right from the start. It is a three-step process. I tell them that when you get the test, I want you to follow this process:

Step 1: Scan the entire test first.

Step 2: Sort the problems into three categories: No-clue-how-to-do them, Maybes (if there is enough time to figure them out), and Yeses (you know how to do them without a shadow of a doubt).

Step 3: Manage emotion and time with care:

- For the ones you absolutely have no clue how to do, cross them out.

- For the ones you know how to do, do those next. Do them carefully enough that you don't rush and make silly mistakes.

- After that, focus all your energy on the ones you can figure out given enough time and do as many of those as you can.

You'd be surprised how many additional points kids can pick up right away. Using this technique, kids will have less test anxiety, be a more efficient test-taker, and they'll feel they're in control of the math test. This skill can be applied to other subjects and as a parent you can teach this skill without knowing any of the math concepts.

Question #12: Did you review tests and go over missed problems?

What parents say:

> "We always discussed tests. For any problem our kids missed, we asked:
>
> - if they understood where and how it went wrong;
>
> - if they read the entire question;
>
> - if they rushed through it;
>
> - if they understood the material?"
>
> "I showed my kids how sometimes a test has a natural progression. Sometimes the answer you get for one problem helps you answer another problem, like when you have to multiply 8 x 7 for one problem, and then later you have to factor 56."
>
> "We also taught them to ask, 'What do I think the teacher will put on the test?' And after a test, we'd compare those guesses to what actually was on the test. My kids figured out that the better they understood the teacher, the better they were at anticipating what the teacher wanted them to learn and know. Some of their teachers would even tell the class, 'Be sure you know this. It will be on the test.'"
>
> "But the most important thing we tried to pass on was: tests are not as important as learning the subject matter. Tests are a chance for you to demonstrate part of what you've learned; learning has to happen first, and

> *the learning is what matters in the long run. Going over the returned tests, we'd look for where there were gaps in the learning, and figure out how to solve the problems they missed on the test. This worked out really, really well, because one final exam was nothing but math questions that students had gotten wrong on previous tests!"*

Here is my experience:

Yes, we did review tests and go over missed problems. My attitude toward bad grades and missed problems is that they are worth their weight in gold. This is because they show us what material needs to be worked on, and moreover, they help kids learn their unique patterns when it comes to their test-taking. Once kids become aware of their unique test-taking pattern it helps them in other classes as well.

When our kids were younger, I initiated this "exam your exam" with them and showed them that, by and large, **there are really only three** *categories* **of mistakes that show up on math tests: foundation holes, careless mistakes, and I-ran-out-of-time**. So we sat together and looked at where they missed points. It was hard for them to figure out which mistake was in which category at first, but we kept on going with this process. Because they had to analyze their own mistakes to see what kind of mistake it was and how many points they lost for each kind of mistake, they learned what they needed to focus on for the next test. Our kids, later on, said this process is like "sharpening their fishing hooks"—hard but well worth the effort.

Embracing and analyzing mistakes is the best way to grow test-taking skills.

Question #13: Did your child have goals? How did he communicate what they were? Were her goals taken seriously? Respected? How did you show your support?

What parents say:

"From a very young age, our oldest son wanted to be a professor. He wants to be the first Ph.D. in the family."

"Our daughter wants a career in music and performance. She asked, 'Why do I need to be good at math? I'll never use it. I want to be a singer!' So my husband asked who her favorite performers are, and she said names like Taylor Swift and Beyonce. He asked if she liked TLC songs, and she said 'Sure.' Then he asked if she knew that many performers end up bankrupt, broke, like the young women of TLC, because they never learned how to manage money. They trust managers to take care of the money for them, and their money disappears. The smart performers learn the math of money, and taxes, and investments, and they not only stay rich, but they also become richer. Suddenly our daughter realized that math DID matter, even to artists. Maybe especially to artists. They started watching biographies together about pop singers, and every time things went wrong with finances, he'd ask, 'Could they have prevented that if they'd paid attention to the math?' She got the idea. And she started really paying attention to math again. And then her music teacher showed the class how music recordings are combinations of wavelengths, and she couldn't wait to study wave equations."

Here is my experience:

When she was five years old, our daughter became fascinated with the stethoscope that a family physician friend gave her for her birthday. She carried that thing around all day long. First, she pretended to listen to her doll's heart just like she'd seen on TV. When our friend came over and showed her where to put it on a live person, she was hooked and declared she wanted to be a doctor. We thought, kids often change their minds; she'll get interested in other things. And she did. For a while, she focused on painting, music, and then tennis. But then she spent a summer in her sophomore year volunteering at a local hospital (doing things that would have terrified me); she dug out that old stethoscope and got serious about medicine again. Because we supported her in math, she was able to qualify for pre-med programs in colleg.

Growing up, our son loved Legos. He'd spent hours building model ships, hospitals, and cities, robots, and airplanes. And Legos are not cheap.

Thank goodness for friends who shared their old ones, and yard sales. As he got older, we were careful to choose schools that had an emphasis on robotic and drafting programs, and we introduced him to our friends who are engineers or who have passions for woodworking or machine shops. He was actively seeking these activities out for himself as well. When he got to high school, he was co-captain of the robotics team as a freshman, and the team went to sectionals in Seattle, Washington. They didn't win that year, but the experience, in his words, "was priceless."

Question #14: Did Math (and MathAbility) help your kids with other classes? If so, how?

What parents say:

> *"Our son hated when he had to learn math proofs, proving each step so that a proof went right back to the first rules of geometry and math. He got so impatient. But then he began listening to TV shows and saying, 'That doesn't follow. That's wrong.' He realized that logic isn't just for math. He is finding it in his other classes, science and literature, and language. And he's noticing when logic is missing in places where it is needed, like when his friends get in fights."*

Here is my experience:

Math and MathAbility helped both our kids tremendously. For our son, math helped him use his imagination for robotic design. As his designs got more complex, he and his teammates started to seek experts outside of their school to guide them. They enrolled in community college classes to learn computer-aided drafting and found internships at the local university's Mechanical Engineering Departments to learn machine shop. They formed an alliance with another team and corresponded with other robotic teams nationwide. The byproduct of enhanced MathAbility gave him the freedom to pursue his passion and connect with other like-minded kids to explore what's possible beyond math.

For our daughter, math helped her develop tenacity, attention to detail, and pattern recognition. When she was a junior in high school, she decided to take up Chinese. Up until then, she had not expressed any interest in learning any foreign language. Chinese is a tough language for any native English speaker to learn, so after about a month when the novelty wore off, she started complaining about copying and memorizing the characters and the subtle intonation differences in pronunciation. When she didn't get the grades she wanted in Chinese, she used the pattern-recognition training from studying math and grouped a bunch of Chinese characters by the way they looked to her. As with studying for math, persistent practice is necessary for learning a foreign language. She applied that and put the notecards everywhere in the house, so that she could practice while she was brushing her teeth, washing her hands by the kitchen sink, and by her laptop when she was chatting with her friends. The tonality change in Chinese pronunciation was subtle but she persisted with her practice, and by the time she finished high school, she felt sufficiently confident to spend a gap year in Shanghai with a Chinese family and hiked the Pacific Crest Trail before starting college.

Question #15: Do you have any advice for taking standardized tests like the PSAT?

Here is my experience:

Yes, start early. Test-taking skills take a long time to build, and the first thing to build up is reading comprehension. The better kids are at reading comprehension, the better they'll be at math, especially word problems, and the better they will do on standardized tests where sometimes even the math questions are asked in a tricky way.

And then there is the Reading Comprehension portion to get through. So, read together. It can be anything, so long as you read it with your kids. What do they like to read? What do they want to read? It can be comics; it can be a book that your kid's favorite movie is based on; it can be a car manual if your teenager wants to be able to drive; it could be a newspaper; it could be their favorite story from childhood. Read together and discuss what you're reading. Ask what unusual words mean. Look up the words you don't know, so your child learns how to use a dictionary, whether it is a book or an online dictionary. Notice how sentences are put together. Pay attention to punctuation: What does punctuation tell you about how to read the words?

Reading comprehension improves PSAT and SAT reading, writing, and math scores. So as early as possible, start reading together and discuss what you are reading.

The next thing is to help your kids recognize that, physiologically, there is very little difference between feeling fear and feeling excited. The hormones are almost exactly the same. But fear makes us shut down, so the goal is to shift from fear by either downshifting to calm or changing gears to the excitement of "Yay, I'm about to take a test and I'm going to bring my best to the test."

Before taking a standardized test for real, help your child get a baseline practice test score, and do this as soon as possible. Sometimes just knowing where they are, even if it is at the bottom, helps relieve the fear of the unknown. Getting an assessment of the baseline helps kids figure out exactly where the deficits are—foundation holes or time management or careless mistakes. For standardized Scantron questions, checking answers, and lining up the bubbled answers to the questions are particularly important skills. When they skip a question on the test, many kids fail to skip the corresponding line on their answer sheet, and they end up putting the right answers in the wrong places.

Also, building good test-taking skills takes practice, practice, and practice, and to do that, you'll need to help your child locate practice tests. There are a lot of free resources to take those practice tests: download them on the Internet, or get a booklet. Then review test results and categorize trouble spots: Is it a lack of knowledge, is it a careless mistake, or is it time management? For example, spending twenty minutes on one problem on a timed test is not the best use of the ninety minutes on that section. Learn to "choose your battles" and answer the maximum number of questions correctly before returning to problems that are troublesome.

In addition, it's important to know what kind of test your child is taking. Some tests, like the PSAT, do not "punish" test-takers for guessing and getting an answer wrong. Other tests are less forgiving and kids actually get docked points for wrong answers. So, every test-taker needs to figure out the best way of dealing with hard questions. Is it better to circle a hard question and its corresponding answer line lightly with a pencil, or leave it blank and get back to it later? Or is it better to make the best guess, checkmark the answer, and review it later if there is extra time?

Lastly, I'll explain something very important to the kids I work with. This is something almost nobody expects. I tell them that when you're trying to practice and learn test-taking skills, it almost always gets worse before it gets better. I want them to know this in advance so they won't give up in despair. For example, if they started with a test score baseline of 500 and after trying to improve skills their next test score is 450, that's okay. It's normal. I tell them: it's because you're spending time and energy on learning new skills, and you have to give up old habits that don't work, and all this effort slows you down. New skills build a little bit at a time, so be patient.

A few more tips: Be conscious of what is optimal for your child. If your kid tests better on an empty stomach, honor that; if a full stomach is better, then a good breakfast is in order. A good night of sleep can really be important.

A few words on the physical environment. Some kids are sensitive to bright lights or flickering fluorescent bulbs; they might benefit from tinted glasses or a cap, something to protect their eyes—but make sure this is not a violation of a school dress code. One school found out the hard way that environmental factors can affect test-taking: their students who took the test after lunch had significantly lower test scores than the morning group because the chlorine bleach used to clean the tables interfered with their problem-solving abilities.

Question #16: How did math figure in the college application process?

Here is my experience:

Visiting colleges they're interested in is an important aspect of helping our kids to narrow down the colleges they were applying to. The road trips proved to be great and memorable bonding opportunities, and college visits helped our kids see their school classes as leading to something, not as an imposition or a waste of time. After talking to many of my math families, we made a point to not just do the usual "here is our beautiful campus tour" on our kids' college trips. We asked tough questions: graduation rates, the percentage of incoming students who did not complete their first year. We also requested to sit in on higher-level classes even if such a request would likely be denied. We were persistent. One benefit of taking higher-level math classes and having their transcripts was that when we took them to visit colleges and universities, both our kids were invited to sit in on classes in physics, chemistry, engineering, and biology during their campus tours. They got to talk to professors and advisors in their potential majors, instead of just being guided by student tour guides. Having solid math grades also helped them stand out on their college applications.

In the next chapter, we will look at *why* helping your kids with homework is so important. Then we will dive into specifics of *how* you can help, even if you are not able to solve math problems.

CHAPTER 9

Help with Homework Even When You Can't Help with the Math

> Give the ones you love wings to fly, roots to come back,
> and reasons to stay.
> —Dalai Lama

This chapter is about helping with your child's homework, but instead of jumping into telling you what to do and what not to do, I'm going to tell you a story first. It's almost a parable. For parents who want advice along the lines of what to do and what not to do, you can skip ahead to the second half of this chapter. It even has checklists. This way, if you want to change how you work with your child or with your child's tutor, you can use the included checklists and guidelines to see if there might be something you haven't considered.

The egg and tomato story

When I was a kid, my mom made a dish that seemed to have just two basic ingredients: eggs and tomatoes. When I think of home and comfort food, this egg and tomato dish is what sums it all up. As I tell you about it, maybe you'll see why it can help you envision how to best guide your child's math journey.

She would start with all the care in the world by choosing the best tomatoes. I can still see her taking each tomato into her left hand and tapping it with her right fingertips, looking for the right softness. Only years later, when I tried to make the dish myself, did I understand that ripeness of a tomato is crucial. Too ripe? The tomato has too much juice and the dish gets watery. Not ripe enough? The tomatoes form hard chunky islands.

She would dice the tomatoes and put them aside in a bowl. She'd take the time to let the eggs come to room temperature and then beat them to a properly foamy state. In a large bowl, she'd add a pinch of salt first, crack the eggs, then beat the eggs. "It's all in the wrist." She'd try to show me, but as a child all I wanted was for her to start the cooking part. To my untrained eyes, the cooking started with pouring oil into a pan.

The temperature of the cooking oil was a mystery to me. My mom would wait ever so patiently, rolling the oil in the pan, over and over. I remember always asking her the same thing: "Why are you not adding the eggs *yet*?" She'd tell me she was looking to see how long the oil sticks to the side of the pan. Years later, I finally figured out that timing determines oil temperature, and that in turn affects the consistency of what she called "half-cooked young eggs," which is the first stage of the recipe. What I found out—the hard way, because as a child I was too impatient to listen—is this: if I dump beaten eggs in before the oil is hot enough, all I get is a flat, lifeless egg pancake; if I dump the eggs in too late, the eggs burn and taste terrible. I remember how hers always slid into the pan with a bit of sizzle, and how she would let them settle, interacting with the heated oil, before she stirred the eggs with a pair of chopsticks so they half-cooked evenly, not just on the bottom. Her eggs always came out partially cooked, still a bit runny, "happy," and perfectly golden.

After she took her happy, half-cooked eggs out of the pan, she set them aside and cooked those diced tomatoes in the same pan. "Don't skip taking eggs out halfway or the dish won't be happy. Timing is the hardest part," she'd say. I remember telling her that the hardest part for me was *waiting*. Somehow, she knew just when enough tomato juice had evaporated to embrace the return of those happy, half-cooked eggs for a perfect blend of yin and yang harmony. The tomatoes would be semi-juicy, their flavor subtly changed by the oil and residual salt from the eggs. What's a semi-juicy state? Just like cooking the eggs and taking them out at the right moment with the right consistency, there was a "baby bear" state for the half-cooked tomatoes between the "mama bear" of too soft and the "papa bear" of too dry. To this day I am not sure how she sensed it: Was it the smell of ripeness? The eye of experience? However she sensed it, she always found the right second to add the eggs back to the half-cooked tomatoes so the eggs finished cooking with tomatoes, fluffy, never burned, and full of flavors. By the time she was ready to plate the dish, I had no patience, no care or hope of ever cooking the egg and tomato dish by myself. All I wanted was to put that egg and tomato mixture into my watering mouth.

A tasty meal and a nurturing homework session have much in common

The reason I tell the egg and tomato story is because a *tasty* meal and a *nurturing* homework session have a lot in common. Can you feel how much my mom's signature dish meant to me, then as a hungry, growing child, and now as an adult who appreciates the love and skills my mom put into making something that nourished me, body and soul? If you can, then you probably can also recognize how much a nurturing homework session can mean to a child, how profoundly it can support a child's developing mind and soul.

A tasty meal doesn't just happen, and neither does a nurturing homework session. And it is not enough to do it just once. Imagine what would happen if we only fed our kids one meal. Homework needs to become as daily as another meal—one that will become a part of your child's being in the same way that nourishing food becomes part of their bones and blood.

Early on, it may be enough to spend ten or fifteen minutes a day on homework, but that will change as kids grow. Establishing *a habit of homework early* is vitally important to prepare a child for the later workload. It is so important that even if your young kid says, "I don't have any homework" or "The teacher didn't assign any" or "I did it already," you still try to make it a practice to sit down with your kid for those ten or fifteen minutes a day. It's easy to let yourself off the hook. (Believe me, I've been there myself more often than I care to admit.) If they say they don't have homework, then spend that time together on some math anyway. Ask them to show you what the teacher taught that day, or go over a recent test. Or do some math foundation practice together, or add up how much money you both spent that day. Do something that uses math.

Why is this so important? Because it shows to your child that *you* take their math seriously. And if you take it seriously early on, the child who loves you and wants your approval and attention will follow suit and take math seriously. And they will have that time with you when nobody and nothing else matters more to you than they do. That means more to a kid than you may realize. Even a child who moans and complains about homework will say, years later, how they loved that time together with a parent, *even while they were complaining*.

And when your kids are older and teachers suddenly start assigning an hour of homework a night, your kids will be ready and prepared. It is much, much easier to go from doing fifteen minutes of homework at night to doing one hour or more of homework a night than it is to go from doing no homework at all to a much heavier workload.

We may see this another way. Have you ever inflated a balloon with your own breath, especially brand-new ones? It can be very difficult to get it to expand. The balloon fights back, the rubber refuses to stretch. Then suddenly it becomes easy, and the balloon gets bigger and bigger until you can tie it off, and there it is. Getting a child to develop a habit of homework practice can feel as oppositional as trying to get that stiff balloon to inflate at first, but once you get past the hump together, you will see your child's life expand with a kind of joy that is born from mastering self-discipline and learning new skills. Also, there is a warning there, in the analogy of a balloon. Trying to make the balloon "just a little bigger" can make it explode. In the same way, pushing a child too hard, trying to make them "just a little smarter" can overdo the learning process, and a child can "blow up" or shut down if their brains get overstretched.

Cooking the eggs and tomato dish and managing homework: the analogy

Now, let's get back to the egg and tomato dish a bit. What was the first thing my mom had to do to make the egg recipe that made my mouth water? She had to have a goal in mind, for starters, and a sense of maternal responsibility, and she had to prepare. No ingredients, no supper. No utensils, no supper. And she needed space to work. So, the first part of helping a child with homework is this: getting ready.

For starters, the right tools for homework—graph paper, pencils, and erasers—are the utensils. You have to have them. Your commitment to your kids' success, your communication skills, and attitude are important ingredients you bring to the recipe. Math skills are like the eggs—the fresher the better. If you don't feel comfortable with your math knowledge, then it will be your child who brings the fresh eggs of the day's lesson. Salt is like patience—it makes everything better. Knowing how to guide them to ask effective questions, and bring a positive attitude are the other 'ingredients' only adults can contribute. And having a dedicated space that everyone keeps clear for homework is the equivalent of a kitchen to cook in.

When I saw my mom assembling the eggs and tomato and bowl and pan, I knew I was in for a special experience. When you take a moment to get in the right frame of mind for homework, to take care of yourself so that you have the energy and mind frame to be patient and calmly supportive, you are letting your child know that something special is about to begin: homework time. You are also showing your child what "care for self so you can care for others" looks like. There is no better way of setting a good example for a child than showing that you respect yourself and take care of yourself. We don't want our kids to grow up to be taken advantage of at work, or by friends, or by partners, but that will happen if they don't respect themselves. When you take that time to settle yourself before you help with their homework, you are showing that self-respect *balances* love for them. Remember when I said that math was about more than math? This is one of those places where becoming strong with MathAbility can be a life lesson.

Organizing how a homework session will go is just like those first preparatory parts of cooking because if you don't do "first things first" in the right order, there would be no supper or at best a mess that no one will enjoy eating. Getting homework off to a good start rests on your shoulders because you are the one who knows how important it is in the long run.

Now let's dive into some details and see how the cooking elements are an analogy for transforming a homework session with your child:

- Assembling utensils, choosing tomatoes, and dicing them corresponds to getting proper materials ready at hand. You had to have already bought them, and now you have to select the ones you need for this homework session and make sure they are ready to use: sharp pencils or mechanical pencils with plenty or refill leads, erasers, sturdy chairs, the graph paper, the homework assignment, and teaching materials, the clear space. The more your kid helps set up and maintain the work area, the better.

- Letting eggs come to temperature—this is having the patience and perception to choose, set, and adjust the time of doing homework together, not when a kid is "cold" with hunger or fatigue. Just as room temperature eggs cook more evenly, kids do better at homework when they aren't worrying about other things, so you may need to help them get to "room temperature" by listening to them tell you about anything that is troubling them, and maybe coming up with a plan to deal with it. This isn't to avoid doing homework; rather, it is to give a child the chance to really focus on math.

- Adding salt (patience) to the bowl *before* you crack the eggs is prioritizing your awareness of what your goal is for the outcome: a *nurturing* homework session, one that "tastes good" in both your memories. With this goal in the bottom of the bowl, before you start cracking any eggs, you will be kinder, more patient, and able to remember the big picture—your relationship with this child, and this child's joy in learning. That also means monitoring yourself. You need patience, kindness, love, and awareness and if you are "out of salt" you need to have your own resources to replace it.

- Beating eggs to a froth is when you ask your child to show what they have learned in class, and discussing how the day's lesson, as well as previous lessons, can help them get through this homework assignment.

- Your parenting skills are what's "all in the wrist," and if you have to build up your wrist strength, you may take parenting classes, or use online or local resources that are in place to help parents.

- Heating the oil to the right temperature is going over the homework assignment (if you feel comfortable) before you dive into problem-solving. Reading through the homework assignment together is warming the pan of your child's mind. Pouring the oil and swirling the oil evenly over the warming pan, that's the two of you making sure your kid's understanding of basic math functions—addition, subtraction, multiplication, division, and the skills the teacher tried to demonstrate before assigning homework—are enough to "cover the pan evenly" so problem-solving won't get too "sticky".

For parents who love math, here are a few additional elements in our analogy:

- Adding the eggs to a hot oiled pan and cooking them just until they are "happy" corresponds to a very important part of doing homework: estimating—half-solving problems before you actually solve them all the way to a correct answer. This stage means you look at every problem in the assignment together and you ask your child, "What math functions do you guess you will need to solve this problem?" Be patient and be firm. Don't let "I don't know" be an answer; you are *encouraging* them to guess, to look at the problem analytically, and to see what they will need to solve it. If it gets silly because they are all the same kind of problem, that's good. It is a teachable moment especially if your child gets impatient and says, "They're ALL the same. Can we move on?" That is when you say, "Ah! You see they are all the same type of problem!" It's okay if your child guesses wrong sometimes; the important part here is to realize that *they* get to be the detective, the problem solver; or that you get to be the detectives together, as a team, like Sherlock and Watson. (You might even start watching or reading detective stories together.)

- Pouring the happy, half-cooked eggs out of the pan is when you've looked over all the problems and figured out how you will try to solve each one. This is also an appropriate time to take a break if your child is tired, hungry, or just needs a break.

- Cooking the tomatoes is where you do the actual one by one problem-solving together. You are "sweating it out" together to "cook" those problems, the diced tomatoes, each one becoming "just right."

- Lastly, when you "put it all together" and make those happy, runny, half-cooked eggs and those semi-juicy half-cooked tomatoes—all your pre-solving estimations and worked through problems—into the perfect homework assignment, you then go over the whole assignment, checking each problem. Did the guess/estimate help? Was it on target? What were the surprises or "sticky bits"? Did checking answers turn up any mistakes? How did any mistakes get made? What happened? What might prevent that same mistake from being made the next time that sort of problem is on a worksheet or test? It is this review that "pulls it all together" in a kid's mind and helps them truly remember the lessons.

My mom's love and skill made a lasting memory and helped prepare me for my life's journey. Your time with your child, doing homework together will do the same in ways you cannot imagine. I'm often reminded that "love—the feeling—is the fruit of love the verb."

Suggestions, checklists, and practical guidelines to help at home or with a tutor

Now that I showed you the beneficial effects that love, preparation, timing, and persistence can have, let's move onto the practical actions when it comes to helping a child with homework even if you can't help with math. The time your kids spend doing math homework is essential to their learning and math success. For most kids' math journey, teachers come and go, but *you* are one constant influence in their lives. In developing the Math And Managing MathAbility (MAMMA) process, I want to help parents obtain a different perspective and shift their focus from "figuring out and doing math" to "developing MathAbility." So this may require a slight shift in your thinking as you look through this section.

Homework time is about *family time*; yet, for many families, homework time, unfortunately, often turns quickly into volatile family time, especially when math gets heavier and denser as kids take higher-level math. *This is why it's so important that you look beyond just "figuring out math," and develop a coherent overall picture of their math journey as early as possible.* This will help **you** stay centered, and do what no other teachers/tutors can do for your child—take charge of their learning environment *and* promptly recognize and properly deal with math-related learning issues. And the best part is that you *can* do this regardless of your own math level.

Kids are reassured when an adult knows what to do and does it: calmly, reliably, without drama, and without making a fuss. Remember in an earlier chapter I shared what I went through with my son and the laundry? It's important to not let a child push your buttons as you set out to establish a productive and effective homework *routine* with them. If you ever find that your child seems positively determined to derail the homework process, take an extra pinch of patience, and remember this: every child I've ever coached has told me they were grateful that their parents made so many efforts on their behalf, *even when the kids themselves acted angry or sullen at the time.*

If their behavior is really difficult, talk it out with them, and see if there is an underlying issue you can resolve together so homework can be about mastering math and strengthening your bond, not power struggles. As you read through the following practical tips, checklists, and guidelines, pick out the low-hanging fruits first; give them a try, and then expand to other items that you think will help your child.

Cultivating a best-odds learning environment

- **Have a large dedicated table**. It's much easier for a kid to concentrate and be productive when all the study materials have enough space to spread out on top of the table. This way, time is spent doing work rather than finding the homework assignment. It may be difficult at first; you may have to clear off a table you've used for your hobbies or as a holding ground for years. You may even, as many of my families have done, need to get a new table and find a place for it.

- **Keep the necessary supplies on hand**. Here is what you will need for homework sessions:

  o A math three-ring binder notebook. With a notebook, you can see all the progression of their work. I find folders are too untidy.

  o Green engineering graph paper for three-ring binders. The green color is calming for most eyes, and the graph lines make it easier to draw and solve certain kinds of math problems, including graphing and geometry.

  o Several sharp pencils and a pencil sharpener, or mechanical pencils with plenty of refills. I'd advise having a separate pencil for everyone who sits at the table. (We'll talk about that a little later on.) If you use regular pencils, I recommend plain ones, not those with decorated outsides, because those are harder to sharpen. But if having a Hello Kitty or Full Metal Alchemist pencil makes math time special for a child, go ahead and use them.

○ Separate erasers. Pencil erasers never last as long as the pencil lead, so have some extra erasers.

○ If the math homework includes geometry, you will probably need a compass set, protractor, and ruler. If you are solving conversion problems, it helps to have both kinds of measuring systems: English rulers and metric rulers, or volume measurement containers.

- **Empty the backpack as soon as the kid gets home.** While it's inadvisable to do homework right after getting home, it *is* advised to empty the backpack right away. This will help the kid get organized and see what homework needs to be done this evening.

- **Have a timer.** This is so you both can see how much time is left. A public timer equalizes adults and kids.

- **Have a way for the child to stop the study session with you.** This could be a physical sign or a card; kids need to feel like they have some power.

- **Have your own reading material or a project to work on.** The message to kids is, "I'm here, but I'm not waiting on you to complete what you need to do. I have something to do that's independent of your work, but I'm here if you need my help." This helps keep a parent from getting fidgety.

- **Minimize interruption.** Make sure everybody else understands that homework time is a special time. It is not a time to interrupt and ask for things. Have a non-verbal way for other kids to ask for attention or help, like a touch on the shoulder, for emergencies. If you have other kids try to demand attention at homework time, pick a quiet time, maybe their bedtime, to listen to them and let them hear you say, "I love you. Your brother/sister needs attention and help. When it's your turn, you will get homework time too."

- **Provide water**. Water breaks can help keep the brain happy and tempers cool. But keep it water, not soda or sugary drinks, and keep it in a closed container. Spills distract kids and break homework momentum.

- **Music**. Allow music if it helps your child concentrate—but only music, not videos, TV, etc. Those are distractions. Instrumental-only music is almost always better than music with words and voices because our brains want to pay attention to anything being said or sung. There are many recordings available online, including music that is supposed to promote concentration and relaxation, such as beta rhythms, or ocean waves, or solfeggio tones. You might find background sounds that help make homework time more pleasant.

- **Calculators**. A child who lets calculators do the work is not learning how to do the math. Even if teachers say it's okay, using calculators to do basic math functions will rob a child of precious practice. Using them to check answers is a help; using them to find answers is like putting a child with healthy legs in a wheelchair. Besides, there are some answers that can only be obtained using fractions or irrational numbers, so using a calculator will actually cause mistakes. Make solving problems without calculators part of the homework process.

    If a child is already "addicted" to calculators, make it a goal to solve at least one problem in each set of similar problems without a calculator. That is the ONLY way your child can prove to you that they understand how to do the math. If they cannot solve even one problem without a calculator, it's almost guaranteed there are problems with the child's math foundation.

- **Who is holding the pencil?** The pencil needs to stay in the child's hand. Always. You can ask questions and you can give explanations, but the child should be doing the work, even if they make mistakes. Learning how to spot and correct mistakes is part of homework. Instead of "saving" a child from making a mistake, wait and see if they can spot it when their answer doesn't solve the problem. If you absolutely need to show something, pick up your own pencil and write with your non-dominant hand to slow down your working tempo. This is your child's homework; let them hold the pencil. Remember: *Teaching calls for this: to let learn.* (Martin Heidegger)

- **Listen more.** Ask your child to explain what they are doing. Ask them what math vocabulary words can help to describe what they are doing. Be patient, they are figuring this stuff out. This is their first time and you've already learned this material.

- **Focus on the right *process*, not the right answer.** Critical thinking is using what you *do* know to figure out how to solve problems that are new but similar to ones you've solved before. It is more important to see patterns and find a method to solve a problem than to rush to the answer. You see, the answer only solves *one* problem; a pattern or process helps you solve *all similar problems.*

- **Keep track of any tricks or shortcuts you learn.** If your child's teacher demonstrates a math trick, shortcut or pattern, it will probably show up in homework and on tests, so look out for them. Tricks are fun to spot, shortcuts save time, and patterns are often the key to a solution. In geometry, for example, there are certain patterns or ratios of right triangles. Kids who can recognize a 3-4-5 right triangle, a 5-12-13 right triangle, or an 8-15-17 right triangle in length-of-sides numbers can solve problems much, much faster than kids who have to use the Pythagorean Theorem every time. Would you rather do lots of multiplying and dividing, or be able to recognize an answer at a glance?

- **Going over quizzes and tests that have been graded**. Reviewing quizzes and tests is a good way to see what a child has learned, and what they still need to figure out. If some problems are still hard to solve, an essential skill may have gotten missed. Or maybe the problems that gave your child trouble on the test seem easy to solve now. But if that happens a lot, there may be test anxiety or other issues that are causing difficulties during test time. If that seems to be a pattern, see if you can figure out together what is making tests harder than they ought to be.

- **Preparing for tomorrow today**. After you get through a homework assignment, preview the next day's lesson. The more you can figure out in advance, the easier the class will be. If you need help understanding the new material, write out one or two specific questions to ask in class.

Practicing these skills will gradually transform homework time into a nightly adventure of discovery, and a time in which a child builds their study skills and their self-confidence. You can be part of that adventure, even if math is not your favorite subject.

Math concepts will get denser and more challenging as your child grows. And it is for this reason that I ask all the parents I come across in my daily life to start building MathAbility early with their kids. Set the foundation of a strong work ethic early. Find the joy in learning together early. Train yourself to do more listening early. Learn to face challenges together early. Do it early because early preparation and planning give you the luxury of time.

Essential Homework Checklists

Supplies

☐ a large, dedicated table

☐ a math three-ring binder notebook

☐ green graph paper for three-ring binders

☐ mechanical pencils, or pencils AND a pencil sharpener

☐ erasers

☐ a timer

☐ a way for the child to stop the study session (a physical sign or a card)

☐ something for the adult to read or a project to work on

☐ water in a closed container

☐ music, if it helps your child concentrate

Actions

☐ Empty the backpack.

☐ Listen more than you talk.

☐ The child holds their pencil. Always. Use a different one if you need to write.

☐ Keep a section for tricks or shortcuts you learn.

☐ Go over quizzes and tests that have been graded.

☐ Prepare for tomorrow's class today.

Tutors: finding the right one for your child, what pitfalls to watch out for, and three ways to work effectively with them

At some point in their math journey, most kids need some form of additional help. This is normal. Finding a tutor is not that hard. But finding the *right* one is. It takes a little more effort. Here are some guidelines, pitfalls to watch out for, and how to work with tutors effectively.

Remember the 80-20 rule using the MAMMA process, knowing math is only 20 percent of an effective tutor. The other 80 percent is finding someone that will help your child *learn how to learn*. When it comes to learning math, we each have a unique style in which we learn best. For example, some kids need to talk to learn. Some kids learn well through stories. Some need a big picture. Some need comfort in the repetition of details. An effective tutor will tune in to your child. This is not always an easy thing, but a little more effort will pay off in a big way for your child's math journey, making it smoother, more pleasant, and successful.

So, what is it like to work with this kind of tutor and what pitfalls should you watch out for? First, the pitfalls: who you normally think is a good candidate may not be a good fit for your child. This is important and worth repeating: who you normally think would be a good candidate is often not. This could be your child's peers, neighbors, cousins who know math, or retired teachers. Just because they know the math doesn't mean they'll be the best fit for your child. Oftentimes people who did not struggle with math cannot appreciate someone who does.

Since knowing math well is only 20 percent of a good tutor, if you're looking for one, you want someone who will be a good communicator, adaptive to your child, *and* can appreciate your child's struggle. That's the important 80 percent. Once you find this person, here are a few suggestions to work with them effectively:

- **Sit in on one or two of the sessions**. Spend some time in sessions so you can see how the tutor interacts with your child. Take no chances.

- **Observe who is doing the most work during the session**. Ask yourself: Who is doing the most writing? If it's the tutor, then your child is not thinking through on his or her own. If your child is doing most of the talking, listen for the quality of the questions. Is it: "I don't get it", or is it more like, "Oh, I see I got stuck on step number three. How did you get there?" The more specific your child's questions, the better; that means they're learning.

- **Give tutors permission to be frank with you**. Ask them upfront to tell you whether they think it's working or not, so your child's math struggle can be addressed elsewhere if needed. Not everybody clicks.

As you can see, there is a little more effort to finding the best tutor for your child than just someone who knows math. Let me encourage you not to think about getting a tutor as something negative; it's really a time to use your child's math struggle as an opportunity to build their confidence and get ahead in their math journey.

Your presence, preparation, love, respect, support, and commitment to nurturing your child's MathAbility really can make the difference between tears, despair, and giving up, or becoming a lifelong learner with good habits, grit, and delight in mastering challenging material. You do not have to know how to do the math to know how to help *them* do the math.

In the next chapter, we will look at what's at the core of math-related conflicts, and how to manage them with ease using the MAMMA process and transform math from tears to smiles.

CHAPTER 10

Handle Math Conflicts that Arise, Especially When Parents Use Math Professionally

> *If I had my child to raise over again, I'd see the oak tree in the acorn more often.*
> —Diane Loomans

Oftentimes, parents who are good at math struggle a bit more when it comes to helping their kids understand math. Over time, the frustration that the parents feel becomes part of the problem—on top of the frustrations and fears that the child is already feeling. If this sounds like your situation, please be encouraged. By remembering and applying MathAbility, you can find a way out of the briars of frustration and cactus thickets of confusion your child has landed in, and help them get back onto the math road. By using the MAMMA process—shifting the focus from "doing the math" to "developing MathAbility"—a family learns together how to solve a real-world problem that resembles a math word problem where the "variables" are people and their different abilities.

To help you visualize the outcome of being a strong family with a happy kid who thrives on math, this chapter has three parts:

1. A case study, examining three elements of math conflicts. This is where parents may find they have "homework" of their own to do.

2. Conflict reduction guidelines and various lists of go-to questions a parent can ask during homework to help a child develop critical thinking skills and ability to formulate effective questions.

3. Voicelessness of a child. What your kids might be trying to say but can't articulate or find the courage to say.

In part one, I'll use a case study to show the three elements that, more often than not, lead to conflicts in the first place. You'll see that by first being aware and then removing those elements, you can help your child not only get homework guidance but also meet their emotional needs *without* getting yourself tangled in frustration. In part two, you'll see how your math knowledge, instead of being a hindrance, can oftentimes be a beacon for your child, illuminating the math landscape. Finally, in part three, you will gain new insight into your child's thought processes and their feelings.

By understanding them and hearing their unspoken words, you can grow closer as you work together to improve their math skills. You'll learn how to help them learn. Better still, by focusing on building MathAbility and learning how to learn with them, your child will have an opportunity to develop and practice life skills of communication, overcoming adversity, and perseverance. Just as math success has a foundation of core learning skills so does success in life. Communication, critical thinking, and grit are foundational life skills.

Part 1. Three elements that often lead to math conflicts, especially when parents are good at math and use it professionally (a case study)

To lead the way out of math conflicts (or better yet, away from conflicts in the first place), we need to first understand the elements of math conflicts. Much in the same way certain elements are necessary for a tornado to form, conflicts around math need certain ingredients to grow into a storm. The top three conflicting-inducing elements are:

- *overwhelming schedule (often involving extracurricular activities);*
- *unchecked energy state before homework session (exhausted parents who work full-time); and*
- *parental expectations that their child should excel at math as they did, and their subsequent frustration.*

To help you see how a combination of those elements leads to math conflicts, let's hear from a professional mom (I'll call her Amy). After our work together, she wrote about her experience with math conflict with her then fourth-grade daughter:

"My husband and I are both scientists and have the technical skills to tutor mathematics to our children and to provide them with homework help. Nevertheless, our daughter struggled with arithmetic and problem solving since the first grade. We tried the Sylvan system, but while it helped her through the third grade, it did not produce long-lasting effects. Our daughter seemed incapable of retaining what she had been taught. By grade four, evenings in our household were marred by frustration over math homework. This frustration manifested itself in various forms from pained expressions to shouting matches… and our daughter invariably ended up in tears.

Dr. Pan patiently explored our daughter's underlying fears with math, her relationships with friends, siblings, teachers, my husband, and myself. Through the sessions with Dr. Pan, I got to know our ten-year-old daughter on an entirely new level—a deeper and more mature level. I gained new insight into her thought processes, her feelings, and genuinely grew closer to her as we worked together to improve her math skills. I feel that I have not only improved my ability to assist my child with math but have become a better parent: I have learned to become more responsive to her needs. I have learned how to help her learn.

The lessons I learned alongside our daughter have been invaluable. I am certain they will last a lifetime."

Element #1: Child's (often crowded) schedule. Amy's daughter loves volleyball, and her school is well-known for its volleyball program. As a result of a grueling tournament schedule, she missed some important math lectures (often the last period of her academic schedule) when her team had to travel out of town. In addition, she was very active in community service. On top of that, she was picked on during her math classes.

Kids sometimes take on responsibilities their parents are unaware of, and they are overwhelmed by stress factors the parents do not know about. When that happens, finding a way forward is like trying to solve a math problem with too many unknowns—you can't do it. This sort of situation IS a real-world math problem, and "solving" it requires finding a shared goal—a common denominator. Each member of the family may have a different numerator, a unique perspective, or sense of purpose, but once everyone agrees on a shared goal, you can all work together.

Overwhelming schedules usually involve extracurricular activities, whether it is team sports, theatre, music, ballet, gaming, or volunteering. And usually, these are vitally important parts of your child's social life. It may be necessary to reduce the number of commitments your child has undertaken, until MathAbility recovers. Please understand this will be terribly painful for your child. They are keenly aware they will be letting down teammates or respected elders, at least temporarily. They may feel a loss of identity or a loss of self-respect. It will be very important to allow your child to keep one or two of these engaging activities. Choosing what to maintain and what to let go of will be a very difficult and very mature choice for your child to make. You can assist with problem-solving techniques, but *your child* has to make the choices.

Element #2: Unchecked energy states before the homework session. Amy ran a large department before she was promoted to be in charge of a school district. Her husband, another highly trained scientist, had his own well-funded research program. While their professional lives were fulfilling, their energy levels during homework sessions were quite drained.

When we started the work together, I gently inquired about their professional workload and provided them with a list so they could do a 360-degree gauge before they sat down to work with their daughter. This checklist helps them to determine just how much energy they have after a full day's work so they can properly determine how many topics they can safely cover without getting caught in frustration themselves:

- *Am I feeling overwhelmed? Tired? Had a rougher day than usual?*
- *Is my child rejecting my message, my method of delivery, or me as a parent?*
- *What topics are on my child's math assignment?*
- *What's my child trying to say?*
- *Will I have the energy to see my kid's point of view regardless of whether it matches mine or not?*
- *If my expectations aren't being met, will I have the energy to see if they're reasonable or not?*
- *Will I have the energy to communicate my expectations in a clear, reasonable manner?*

After the self-gauge list above, I then asked them to gauge their daughter:

- *Is my child under stress—maybe she had a pestering friend with whom she was having trouble, a test or project she's more worried about, a tournament or recital she needs time to practice for?*

Next, I asked them to glance over the homework assignment in its *entirety*:

- *Is it long?*
- *Can I explain the material to my own grandma even in my tired state?*

Element #3: Ineffective Communication To address the third element of ineffective communication from their daughter, we taped a few sessions of roleplay. I have observed that kids with parents who are good at math often feel powerless and find it extremely difficult to communicate what they don't understand. I call this phenomenon "the voicelessness of a child." And their parents, because of their high math aptitude, often cannot appreciate the math struggle their kids are experiencing.

To help with this, I tell parents that if you want to hear your child's "math voice," you have homework to do. You need to hear your own voices. What are you saying, or not saying, to yourself and to your family? Are you expressing, or bottling up feelings of frustration, or fear, or anger, or terrible disappointment? What about the love and hope buried under this avalanche of feelings? It may help to write out your feelings, especially any expectations you have that your child should be good at math, just like you. These expectations and fears are what you bring to every homework session.

Part 2. Conflict reduction guidelines and go-to questions: how to best pass on your math knowledge without conflict

When I work with parents, especially those who are good at math, there are two guidelines and a set of questions I pass onto them. While they are generally effective with all parents, the questions are especially important to parents who are good at math. You may want to pass on your math knowledge to your child, but you may have to "let go" and allow them space and time to develop math skills and math knowledge in a way that is different from yours. This is most especially true when children have a learning style that is different from their parents. A parent may be a logical or a visual learner, while their child is a hands-on or audio learner, or vice versa. When this is the case, it is the parent's responsibility to switch to the child's preferred style of learning.

Guideline #1: Accept full responsibility. When a conflict occurs, an adult who accepts full responsibility for their behaviors also takes ownership of finding a solution. At the same time, there is an opportunity to empower the child by looking for ways to solve the problem together. Since both parent and child are in it for the long haul, it is up to the parent to be patient. As a parent, you can show how much you care by listening quietly. Even when kids are disagreeing, they are still engaged. In these cases, quiet listening keeps the child from disengaging and withdrawing from the relationship, and from doing homework. The most important task during disputes is to maintain the relationship.

Guideline #2: Emotional anchors. When a storm hits ships at sea, they drop an anchor, so they won't be blown away and lost. When homework sessions get stormy, you the parent need to find an anchor: some item or action or quote that will pause the conflict long enough so that you can steer away from a dangerous place where that bond with your child is weakened or on the verge of being broken. This could be a baby photo, a good memory, or a funny joke. Anything that will momentarily bring up a happy emotion. I've had one parent tape Viktor Frankl's quote on the table where she works with her kids: "Between stimulus and response, there is a space. In that space is our power to choose our response. In our response lies our growth and our freedom."

When an emotional anchor is dropped, it's like pressing the pause button in the middle of a movie. This gives both parent and child a chance to reset their feelings, escape spiraling emotions, and get back to a positive interaction. We have the ultimate control over what we say, and we need to remember this in order to take advantage of that control and manage the situation.

Conflict reduction practices and go-to questions

You can't make kids understand math if you just pound on them with math they don't get in the first place. Instead, it's much more helpful to be a math detective of sorts, especially if you're good at math and have not struggled with it much yourself. This often helps to avert the power struggle in the first place. I'd also encourage you to not assume what your child should know by now, or that they know how to ask a clear question.

When working with your kids, try to get a feel for your child's math foundation and address foundation holes if you detect them. I often give parents a list of go-to questions if they are qualified, math-wise; when they sit down with their kids at homework time, I ask them to pay close attention to see if their teaching style is matching their kids' learning style:

- *Are you still following me? If not, where did I lose you?*
- *Which step are you stuck on?*
- *Are you ready to try on your own with a different problem?*
- *Are we going too fast for you?*
- *Do you see the math pattern?*

- *Can you describe it to someone else (say your best friend)?*
- *Learning / teaching style mismatch?*
- *Do you need to see it, talk through it, watch me do it? Do you want me to watch you do it and then we go over it together?*
- *Do you need a definite timeline to do homework sessions?*

As they say, *teaching calls to let learn*, so your patience and gentleness are the foundation to a harmonious knowledge transfer. In addition to the guidelines and checklist, here are a few more hard-earned practices that can help prevent conflicts, or lessen them when they do arise, so you can get through them easier, get over them sooner, and not get defeated by them. As we are the adults in the relationship, it falls to us to say "sorry" first if we were wrong, to listen first, to interrupt less, and to provide anchors that promote stability.

Prior agreements. If you work on math with your child often, then create "rules of engagement," before conflicts occur. This can better prepare you both to weather conflicts when they do arise. Writing out prior agreements and having a copy in the homework notebook is a constructive way to go.

Validate a child's point of view. To reduce conflict, acknowledge the viewpoint of the child. It can be difficult to understand what kids are saying, what they're thinking, and it may take some work, but when children feel they are finally heard, the defenses can come down and constructive engagement can begin.

Special note about crying. Frustration can lead to crying. Crying isn't necessarily a bad thing. It releases pent up energy and relieves pain. Sometimes you help most by just letting a crying spate work itself out. When it's over, look for a way to acknowledge how much you appreciate that this child felt safe enough to show their feelings. And then they can drink some of that water you keep handy, to replace the water they just lost.

Have a few phrases handy to help a kid transition from frustration back to making a mindful effort. As you work to establish ground rules and limits, ask your child what they'd like to hear if they get upset. If they get to help pick the words, they know you have been listening to them. Some phrases to use might be:

- *Do you feel ready to try again?*
- *Let's both take a deep breath.*
- *Tell me a joke. (Laughter is sometimes the best "reset.")*

Have the courage to admit defeat to preserve the relationship. Finally, after trying everything and frustration still sets in for both you and your child over math, then you need to step back and assess the situation. Take a deep breath and zoom out to the big picture: there is always someone else who can teach the math concepts. It may be enough to be that shoulder for your kid to cry on. Remember that your relationship is more precious than getting through a word problem that involves two trains traveling in opposite directions.

Take advantage of local and online resources. Most communities have conflict resolution centers. Take a class. There are wonderful books and podcasts available to help parents process conflict-causing behaviors. Here a few of the favorites that I use with many families where I live:

- *Old Pueblo Mediation Center*
- *Our Family Services*
- *University of Arizona Life and Work Connections*

As our kids mature into adulthood, they become their own individuals with their own values, principles, and ways to interpret events around them. If adults model mutual respect in handling conflicts, math-related or otherwise, kids learn acceptance, resilience, and social grace.

Part 3. Voicelessness of a child: what your kids might be trying to say but can't find the right way to say

As promised in Chapter One, I'm going to help you hear your child's unspoken words. Hearing is what happens when our ears perceive sound; it simply happens. Listening is something you consciously choose to do. It requires concentration, so your brain can process meaning from words and sentences, and also recognize what a child is not saying but wants to get across. Listening leads to understanding, which leads to better communication, which leads to getting over obstacles and learning. Here are some of the most common messages from kids that parents don't always hear but are being communicated if the parent listens:

- *Please be patient with me.*
- *Accept me the way I am.*
- *See my point of view.*
- *I know I'm just an average math student, can you see my other gifts?*
- *Don't compare me to a smarter kid.*
- *Be there for me if I ask you to.*
- *Hear what I'm asking for.*
- *When I fail, don't judge me.*
- *Let me make my own mistakes, but be there if I fail.*
- *Spend time with me; we don't have to plan every minute.*
- *Let me know it's okay to fail as long as I try, and I learn from failure.*
- *Hold me accountable to my word.*
- *Tell me that you'll love me even when I mess up.*
- *Don't show me off to your friends if I get good grades, and don't complain about me if I fall short of your expectations.*

One of the most effective methods I use at work is videotaping role-reversal sessions to help kids speak up. A parent can suggest that the child mimic what the adult does during a conflict. This can be an eye-opening experience. Next, the child can model how they wish mom or dad behaved and spoke instead. Be sure to go into this with a good sense of humor and a light heart. Role-reversal and acting are ways to see our behaviors in a safe way—sometimes we end up laughing at ourselves. After you've seen and heard how your child sees you and hears you, do a reset and act out how you wish you'd done it right the first time. Modeling better ways of behaving and communicating will constructively de-escalate a conflict. The next two composite letters from the kids' point of view are the result of those sessions. They are probably what your kids wish to say if they could fully express themselves.

Letter #1 is a composite demonstrating that young kids often do not have the words to tell you how they feel. Even if they do, they can be too scared to say, "I'm afraid of failing," and "If I do fail, am I going to lose your love?" After many years of working with kids and their families, I put together a letter of what a voiceless child might say when they are hunched up, looking down, twisting their hands, not saying anything, or crying over math. Their unspoken words might sound like this:

Dear Mom,

I know you love me. I also know you think math is important for me to get good at. I know you worry that, without good math grades, my life choices will be limited. I get all that.

This is what I don't get. I don't get why math is so hard for me. I don't get why my math teacher picks on me. I don't get why my friends don't want me in their math study group. It's not like I don't work hard on it. I do. But Mom, the thing that hurts me most is that I don't get why you don't seem to believe that I try.

Math makes me confused, lost, and scared. I don't like to let you down. I know you try to hide your anxious look, but I can tell you are bothered by my test grades. Some of my friends ditch their last class to get home early so they can take the report cards out of their mailboxes. Some even change the report cards. I thought about doing that too. But I didn't because I know you would be more disappointed if I lied than at my bad grades.

I cry a little each time I hear you tell your friends that my brother is the brainy one, or my brother will go far. I look up to him, and I want to make you proud, too. I know he looks down at me and my math questions. I heard him joke with his friends about my dumb questions. It hurts.

I don't feel safe around math now. I seem to get lost all the time, and the harder I try the worse I do. Maybe, like you, I'm just not good at math. Didn't you say that your math teacher picked on you? I try to be polite with my math teacher, but sometimes I feel like the word LOSER is tattooed on my forehead. Just the other day after handing my test back to me, he told the whole class that some people just don't belong in his class.

I got an F on that last test. I don't want to hide it from you, but I'm so afraid that you'll get mad at me.

I'm sorry, Mom. I will try harder.

I just wish I knew how.

Letter #2 is a composite of older kids. In this age group, fear often morphs to anger, and their tender wish to please you sours to frustration. Here is what a teenager might be feeling when they are not talking to you, or when they're swearing aloud, or even shouting, "You don't understand me!" or "Leave me alone!"

Look, Mom, I hate math.

I'm no good at it, and I never will be.

It's too late for me.

Everyone else will go to college or get good jobs and I'll be left behind with the other losers. There is nothing to look forward to, so I just tune everything out.

Don't talk to me, don't try to fix anything.

You'll only make math worse and draw the teacher's attention to me.

I'll never be as good as my younger brother or older sister!

The world is so messed up that even if I was good at something as hard as math, what's the point? And you know the worst thing about math? It spoils everything.

I used to like science. But now instead of learning cool stuff, it's nothing but algebra day in and day out. Chemistry is algebra. Biology is math with graphs and charts. Physics is all wrapped up in word problems.

Math dragged all my grades down. They are so bad now the coach won't even let me try out for the team.

*I remember when you said: "Geometry will be DIFFERENT!" Yeah, I even started to believe you, too. But it's just more *#%$* Algebra disguised as finding angles. And have you seen the next semester's trig? I can't even read the equations, let alone solve them.*

I know you tried to help. But you don't understand how math works, and the parts you do remember you don't know how to teach me. Dad and I just get into more fights. It's so humiliating to ask for help every single step! You told me to ask the teacher for help, but he says he's too busy unless I come during his free period, but I have another class then so I can't.

It's like once you get tall no one likes you for yourself anymore, they only want you to do things, and what you do is never good enough. There's always more tests, more failures, and it never stops, it never gets easier, and I feel like I'm being rushed to someplace I don't want to go and never chose.

I'm just no good at math. Can we not talk about it anymore? Please?!

These older kids feel frustrated, disappointed in themselves, and frightened about their future. They are hurting because of math, and they are shutting down or lashing out. If you can understand that most of their terrible anger is not really against you (even when it sounds that way), and if you can remember that all struggle is temporary, and that you can stay balanced within yourself, then let them vent and ask them what they are most upset about, what is really eating their heart out. If they can trust you enough to finally say it out loud, that is a kind of relief, especially if you still love them after they've let the poison out of their math wounds. The wounds are still there, but now there is a chance they might heal. You might be able to pick the one thing that bothers them most and come up with a conditional plan to remedy it. Maybe you, as a parent, can get a teacher or administrator to take your child seriously and make sure they get help addressing whatever math foundation holes are derailing your kid. Even if you cannot help them solve the algebra problems, you will be showing your child that you care, you are on their side, and you are willing to fight for them.

And if together, you can remedy even one of the problems that are overwhelming your child, it is wonderful how much that relief can make all the other problems less terrible, less unbearable.

Letter #3 contains words we might hear even though they often go unspoken, from the no-longer-a-child we helped nurture and unfold. Remember I shared earlier about my daughter's math journey? This one is not a composite letter. It's actually from my daughter who is finishing up her junior year at Washington University in St. Louis:

> *Hey Mom,*
>
> *I'm in college studying biomechanical engineering right now and am taking my last math class. Fingers crossed but it looks like that when this semester's over, I'll have never gotten any Bs in college math!*
>
> *I remember panicking the first time I saw vectors because they didn't make any sense. Thanks for helping me even when I didn't want it in grade school. Right now, a lot of things don't make sense right away, but I've learned that's OK. All I need to do is go through a problem slowly, ask for help if needed, and everything turns out fine.*
>
> *The best help you provided at home was taking me out to ice cream the first time I got an F on that math exam. If I could go back in time, I'd agree with you and tell myself that a bad grade does not mean I'm dumb or stupid.*
>
> *Math is one of my favorite classes right now. I enjoy how straightforward and logical it is. Calculus and differential equations are incredibly useful and show up in all of my classes, preparing me for studies in medical school. I think it's really cool how differential equations can describe how our bodies work.*
>
> *Thank you from the bottom of my heart!*

So you see, it can get better. YOU can make a difference, first by role modeling your appreciation for math if you use them professionally, second by role modeling maturity and good communication skills, and third by helping your child to learn how to learn and how to solve life problems. Wherever you are in this crazily fulfilling job called parenting, please know that you are loved and appreciated. It may take a while to unwind conflicts that have been years in the making, but this is how you restore your family's relationship foundation.

In the last chapter, as our journey together is about to end, I'll tell you one last story about my mom's advice on how baking bread is like raising happy kids—happy math kids in particular. And I'll also share with you what's happening on my end and how you can join our growing Door-2-Math family online.

CHAPTER 11

Baking Math Pi(e)

With family on graduation day, Circa 2002

This chapter about finding balance between doing too much and not enough for our kids when it comes to their math. Since I can't bake to save my life, I found it a bit amusing that one of the most helpful pieces of parenting advice I ever received from my mom is on baking. And I hope it'll help you too.

When our first child was born, my mom gave me one piece of advice that served and continues to serve me well. She said that joyful parenting is essentially *helping* to bring unlimited possibilities—embodied inside another human being— to full bloom. "It's going to be a laborious process," she said, "but very rewarding—not unlike a baker making bread from scratch and releasing all the potential in the flour."

"But Mom, you know I can't bake!" Looking at the tiny pink-cheeked baby girl in my arms, I remember feeling that panic inside my chest (and still do, even though my daughter is about to graduate from college).

"Just be ready to raise yourself first," Mom said. "Your daughter will do the rest of raising you." It sounded absurd back then. But looking back some twenty-odd years, my kids did raise me more than I raised them. They made me a better human being—calmer, more humble, more persistent, and *infinitely* more patient. The love and devotion required to share a pleasant journey with my kids have transformed me.

Over the years, I've often thought of my mom's advice like parenting to baking bread. If a parent is too much of a doer and opens the oven too often, the bread can't rise properly; too little of a doer and too much of a sideliner, the dough doesn't get kneaded properly and the bread can't expand to its full potential. So, doing not enough for our kids starves their growth, but doing too much can be harmful. Finding the right balance of doing just enough for each child is indeed a long, drawn out journey and a laborious process.

Yet how rewarding is it to see them becoming self-assured young adults, especially when they set off for college with a bright future ahead of them? Now both of our kids are out of the house, and we're officially empty-nesters. Remember those two TED talk questions I mentioned earlier? If you ask if I still try to answer them at night? Yes. Do those two questions still tug at me at night? Yes.

Did I teach enough to my child?

How much contribution will my child remember?

If pressed, my answer is the same as my mom's: "Wrinkles mean you laughed, grey hair means you cared, and scars mean you loved."

As to those asking why this chapter title of is spelled "pie" with an "e" in parentheses, my answer is that *pie without ego tastes better*. And, just like the number pi, the process of baking "math-pi" with a kid is just as irrational[12] and never-ending…

What's next?

Here we are—our journey is about to end here. We've done a lot together. Thank you for getting this far with me. Now let's talk about what is next for you as a parent or guardian, for me, and, to a certain extent, for our Door-2-Math community.

I want you to experience the power of helping your child. Albert Einstein once said, "Information is not knowledge. The only source of knowledge is experience." Reading a book is great, but only a great starting point. Come back and reference this book's checklists and roadmaps. And be sure to check out our seven-day challenge.

Seven-day challenge

As you and your child take this MathAbility journey, I want to help. I have created a free, seven-day follow-up email series for you to keep on receiving tips, stories, mini-quizzes, and best practices to help you put all the information in this book into action. You'll get all seven email challenges when you sign up for your Digital MathAbility Toolbox for Parents at www.FromTearsToSmiles.com.

---

[12] **pi**—which is written as the Greek letter for p, or π—is the ratio of the circumference of any circle to the diameter of that circle. Regardless of the circle's size, this ratio will always equal **pi**. The decimal value of **pi** is a never ending, non-repeating number (called irrational number) and it's approximately 3.14…

All this is just a fancy way to say: if you take a pipe cleaner, first measure its length, bend it into a circle and then measure the widest part of the circle you just made. The length of the widest part of the circle is always about ⅓ of the length of the wire you started with. No matter what the length of the wire you started, this (ratio) is always true.